THE PASTA MACHINE COOKBOOK

THE PASTA
MACHINE
COOKBOOK

GINA STEER

FIREFLY BOOKS

A FIREFLY BOOK

First published in Canada in 1997 by
Firefly Books Ltd
3680 Victoria Park Avenue
Willowdale, Ontario M2H 3K1

Canadian Cataloguing in Publication Data
Steer, Gina
Pasta machine cookbook

Includes index
ISBN 1-55209-162-7

1. Cookery (Pasta).   2. Pasta products.
3. Pasta machines.   I. Title.

TX809.M17S73 1997   641.8'22   C97-930681-7

Creative Director: Richard Dewing
Art Director: Clare Reynolds
Designer: Isobel Gillan
Project Editor: Clare Hubbard
Editor: Barbara Croxford
Home Economist: Gina Steer
Photographer: Philip Wilkins, except pages 20, 22, 23
and main jacket image by David Armstrong

Typeset in Great Britain by
Central Southern Typesetters, Eastbourne
Manufactured in Singapore by
Pica Colour Separation Overseas Pte. Ltd.
Printed in Singapore by
Star Standard Industries (Pte.) Ltd.

Picture Credits
Life File: pages 7, 19, 28, 40, 59, 76, 93;
Peter Wilson: pages 105, 121.

The publisher would like to thank
O.M.C. MARCATO s.r.l. for supplying the Atlas Regina
Extruder machine featured on pages 8 and 25.

CONTENTS

INTRODUCTION

There are few greater pleasures in life to me than eating. I am sure most people would agree with this, and perhaps one of the greatest and most versatile of all foods has to be pasta. From being the staple diet of all Italians, pasta has quickly become popular everywhere, evolving over the years from just simple noodles or ribbons to the many different shapes, colors, and flavors which we all now enjoy—offering the most wonderful taste sensation to all discerning palates.

There are two main types of pasta—flour and water pasta and egg pasta. Flour and water pasta is made from durum wheat flour (a high gluten flour, called semolina in Italy), and these pastas include the ever faithful spaghetti, tubes, such as rigatoni, and many other shapes which complement strong, spicy, zesty sauces.

Then there is egg pasta, which is made from flour and eggs. The flour used here is a soft wheat flour which, outside Italy, is equivalent to an all-purpose flour. However, there are some who say that durum wheat flour must be used for both kinds of pasta and, in some areas of Italy, olive oil and salt are added. Egg pastas absorb sauces far more readily than the flour and water pastas, and are well suited to egg, butter, and cream sauces. Egg pasta is very delicate with a thin texture. It is, therefore, important when making this pasta to keep the pasta warm during the making and handling. The best way to store it is to let it dry completely and then keep at room temperature in jars.

Although there are many commercially made pastas available, many cooks enjoy the challenge of making their own pasta, as the flavor and texture of homemade pasta is far superior to store bought. Owning your own pasta-making machine takes much of the hard work and effort out of the job and helps to make homemade pasta far more achievable. They are simple to use and, once the basic techniques have been mastered, you will be able to make the most delicious pasta meals with great expertise and very little effort.

As well as a pasta-making machine, there are a few other basic pieces of equipment and tools that you will need when making homemade pasta (see page 9). They are all easily obtainable from kitchen stores or large department stores. You will most probably find that you already possess most of them in your kitchen.

There are a few simple techniques that are vital for a successful result and, providing you follow these techniques when you first embark on making your own pasta, I guarantee that you will not fail in serving delicious pasta every time.

CHAPTER ONE

PASTA KNOW-HOW

BEFORE YOU BEGIN MAKING YOUR PASTA MAKE SURE YOU KNOW HOW TO USE YOUR MACHINE CORRECTLY AND THAT YOU HAVE ANY OTHER NECESSARY EQUIPMENT AT HAND. THIS CHAPTER WILL EQUIP YOU WITH THE BASIC KNOWLEDGE TO GET YOU STARTED, INCLUDING A GUIDE TO THE ESSENTIAL INGREDIENTS THAT YOU NEED TO MAKE DELICIOUS PASTA DISHES.

Pasta Machines

When using your pasta machine for the first time, don't expect a perfect result; like everything, practice makes perfect, but the results amply justify the effort.

There are many different pasta machines available on the market. Some simply roll out the pasta dough and cut it into varying ribbon widths; there are attachments available for these machines for making other pastas such as ravioli and cannelloni. Other machines actually mix the pasta dough and have many attachments for making an assortment of shapes as well as ribbons and ravioli. Some are electrically operated, some are hand operated. In all cases it is vital that the manufacturer's instructions are thoroughly read before using your machine for the first time as the machines vary slightly. In this book we have tried to show you the main types of machine that are available in kitchenware stores and department stores, and we have given you the essential information so that, no matter what type of machine you have, the pasta you produce will be perfect.

Using Your Hand-operated Machine

Before using your machine for the first time, wipe down thoroughly with a clean cloth to remove any excess oil. After you have finished using your machine, wipe down with a clean, soft, dry cloth or, if preferred, brush with a soft brush. With regard to the rolling and cutting machine, **never, never** wash in detergent or water as the intricate parts will not work properly. If excess pasta has dried on the machine, just knock lightly and the pasta will fall off. **Take care** with the cutter section as this is a separate section of the machine and should be removed for cleaning and to prevent it falling off accidentally.

Never insert knives or sharp points in between the rollers. If desired, the ends of the cutting rollers can occasionally be smeared with a little oil if they are sticking slightly.

Below A hand-operated extruder machine cuts different pasta shapes depending upon which cutter you attach.

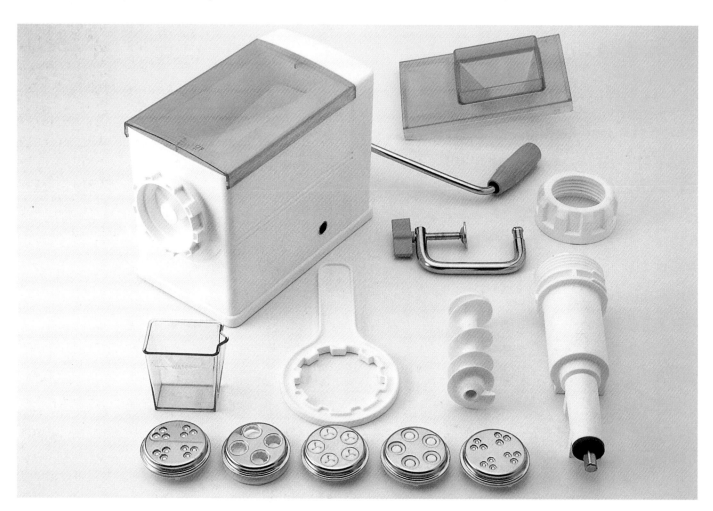

ELECTRICALLY OPERATED MACHINES

When using your electrically operated machine for the first time, **read the instructions** before you do anything else. Unpack the machine and check that it is complete. The machine should not be used by children, and remember **never** leave the machine plugged in when not in use or when cleaning or carrying out any maintenance. If in doubt, contact your nearest stockist or an authorised dealer.

Ensure that the plug on the machine is correctly fitted—that the earthing of the socket is correct and the power supply corresponds to the data on the machine.

Never try to remove the extruder when in use—a safety device is fitted to ensure that the machine will not work when the lid is removed, so it is important to ensure that the machine is assembled correctly before switching on.

Thoroughly clean the machine after use; wash all parts that come into contact with food.

Below An electrically operated pasta machine.

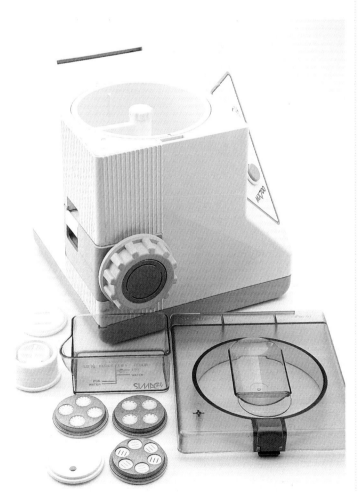

Make sure the machine has a thermostat fitted which will automatically switch off the machine if it overheats. Normally, after 15–20 minutes it will start up again. If the machine has been in operation for more than 25 minutes, this may result in the machine switching itself off.

When using any of the extruders, immerse in hot water, then dry thoroughly, and fit to the machine. To clean the extruders after use, immerse in hot soapy water, leave to soak for a few minutes, then with a hard bristle brush knock out any food residue. Dry thoroughly.

When mixing in the machine, it is important to use the correct quantity of flour and liquid (**refer to recipe given in manufacturer's instructions**). The slide must always remain in the machine and the mixture should be neither too wet nor too dry. When beginning to use the machine, the first batch extruded can be irregular in shape until the machine has warmed up.

EQUIPMENT

Dough Scraper—this is made from plastic or metal and is ideal for scraping the sticky dough off the work surface before kneading, prior to rolling.
Fork—this is just an ordinary fork which is used to mix the flour and eggs together to make the pasta dough.
Grooved Wooden Butter Shaper—this is used to give the ridged effect on pasta shapes; a wooden pencil or piece of dowel is also used to make tubes.
Pastry Cutter—used for cutting out filled ravioli, if you do not have the ravioli cutter for your machine. Also used for cutting lasagna sheets.
Cookie Cutters—plain or fluted, for cutting out rolled pasta when making tortelloni, etc.
Kitchen Knife—used for cutting, chopping, etc.
Grater—used for grating or shredding cheese.
Large Saucepan—you will need a very large saucepan as pasta needs to be cooked in plenty of boiling water.
Colander—ideal for straining the cooked pasta. If preferred, you can use a draining spoon for removing stuffed pasta.
Dish Towels—you will need some clean dish towels so that the rolled pasta shapes or filled pastas can be left to dry before cooking.
Plastic Wrap—this is required to wrap the prepared pasta dough to prevent it from drying out before filling.
Food Processor—this can be used if desired to make the dough, although you will still need to knead the dough.

PASTA CATALOG

There are many different pasta shapes, colors, and flavors available and one would need a book by itself to list every single one that is made, both in and out of Italy; also, many pastas have different names depending on which region of Italy you are in. Listed below are the most commonly known and used pastas including shaped pastas that are easy to make in your pasta machine or by hand once you have used your machine to roll out the dough.

LONG AND RIBBON PASTA

The most well known are perhaps spaghetti, fettucine, and tagliatelle. Most sauces served with long pastas contain small pieces of food rather than large chunks. This is so that the sauce ingredients cling to the pasta when it is twirled on a fork. But, of course, this is only a general rule and rules are made to be broken.

LONG PASTA

Angel Hair *(Capelli D'Angelo)* **(1)**—an extremely fine, long pasta, very light and delicate in appearance. Ideal if served with a broth and makes an ideal pasta to serve as a dessert.

Spaghetti (2) (can also be called vermicelli)—the best known of all pastas, commercially available in a wide range of colors.

Spaghettini (3)—the "ini" at the end of pastas means small, so this pasta is smaller or thinner than spaghetti.

RIBBONS

Fettuccine (4)—narrower than tagliatelle: $1/5$ inch wide. Perfect for both appetizers and main courses.

Pappardelle (5)—a wide pasta about $3/4$ inch wide.

Tagliatelle (6)—about $1/3$ inch wide. Comes from the Italian word *tagliare*: "to cut." Perhaps one of the most well known of the ribbon pastas. Ideal with rich, meaty sauces.

Taglioni (7)—a very narrow pasta about $1/16$ inch wide.

PASTA SHAPES

There are an immense variety of special shaped pastas, all designed to catch the eye and appeal to our aesthetic senses. However, there is another role of the shaped pastas and that is to entrap more of the delicious sauces that are put with the pasta and thus increase our enjoyment while eating. Many of the shapes that are now available are commercially made. I have listed here the most popular shapes to try, using a pasta-making machine.

Brandelle (8)—ragged or torn small pieces of pasta dough.

Farfalle (9)—bow ties or butterflies.

Fusilli (10)—spiral shapes.

Garganelli (11)—an irregular shaped tube with jagged edge, traditionally made by hand.

Macaroni (12)—hollow tubes of pasta, larger than spaghetti.

Maltagliati—irregular shapes of pasta, cut out with a pastry cutter.

Orecchiette (13)—or "little ears."

Penne (14)—perhaps the most well known of tubes. Difficult to make by hand if you do not have a machine that actually makes and shapes penne. A good substitute for penne is garganelli, which is simpler and quick to make by hand. There is little difference in the look except that garganelli is more irregular.

Rigatoni (15)—Ridged tubes, like large ridged macaroni. Good for baked dishes.

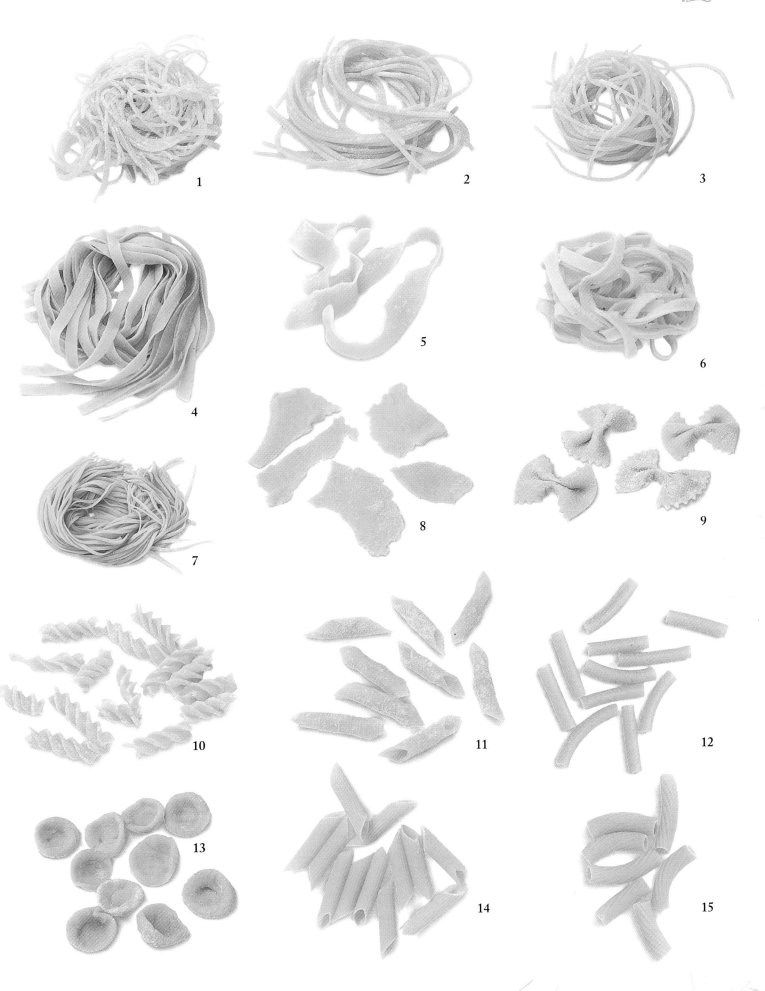

1

2

3

4

5

6

7

8

9

10

11

12

13

14

15

FILLED PASTAS

Filled pastas incorporate cannelloni, lasagna, ravioli, and tortelloni.

Cannelloni—sheets of lasagna that are stuffed and rolled, topped with a sauce, and baked. Can be made using an attachment to your machine or by hand.

Lasagna—flat sheet of pasta about 5-inches wide. Layered with meat, fish, or vegetable sauce, often topped with cheese and baked.

Ravioli—small squares that are filled with a variety of different fillings, cooked, and served tossed in a sauce (see page 24 to make). Can be made using a special attachment for your machine or by hand.

Tortelloni—similar to ravioli, often filled with Swiss chard or spinach and ricotta cheese. Can be similar to cappelletti, made from a round of pasta.

COLORED AND FLAVORED PASTAS

Colored and flavored pastas are more popular outside Italy. The only colors that can normally be found in Italy are red tomato pasta and green spinach pasta (*pasta verdi*). Colored and flavored pastas are easy to make and are an interesting and attractive alternative. (See pages 94 to 104 for recipes.)

Green—Spinach Pasta—also known as *verdi*. Made by adding finely chopped spinach. When rolled with the machine, the color is very even.

Orange/Red—Tomato Pasta—made by adding tomato paste to the basic dough.

Yellow—Saffron Pasta—made by adding saffron strands.

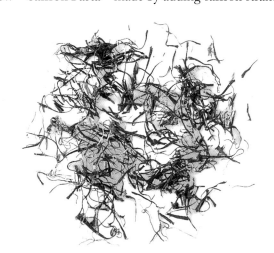

Brown—Mushroom Pasta—made by adding finely chopped, soaked, dried mushrooms.

Black Pasta—made by adding squid ink.

Red—Beet Pasta—made by adding beet purée.

Brown—Chocolate Pasta—made by adding semi-sweet chocolate and sometimes unsweetened cocoa powder.

Herb Pasta—made by adding finely chopped fresh herbs.

Citrus Pasta—made by adding freshly grated lemon, lime, or orange rind, or a mixture of all three.

Pasta Larder

Some ingredients are so synonymous with pasta that I would not dream of being without them when cooking any pasta dish. Here I have listed the main ingredients that you can expect to find in this cookbook with simple explanations where necessary.

Oil and Vinegar

Extra Virgin Olive Oil The finest of all oils, ranging in color from pale green to deep yellow, depending on the growing area and the olives used. It is made from a single cold pressing of the olives. Best used for dressings rather than sauces, as it would be wrong to heat extra virgin olive oil and risk losing its fine flavor and aroma.

Virgin Olive Oil A very fine oil but it does not quite have the same flavor and aroma as extra virgin olive oil. Better to be used for dressings or in sauces which do not have strong flavors and are only briefly heated so that the flavor of the oil comes through.

Pure Olive Oil A blend of refined olive oil and virgin olive oil, and is the cheapest of the three. It is better suited for cooking as the flavor is less overpowering and does not conflict with the other ingredients.

Balsamic Vinegar The king of all vinegars that has been matured in oak caskets for up to 50 years. Use sparingly; its fine, full flavor goes a long way.

Ham

Pancetta Air-cured ham with the addition of spices, used a great deal in Italy. If pancetta is unavailable, lean smoked bacon can be used.

Parma Ham It is the fat from Parma ham that is so useful in sauces. Normally sold cut very thinly, an air-dried ham with a very distinctive flavor.

Prosciutto An air and salt-cured ham, aged for one year, that can be used in place of Parma ham.

CHEESE

ABOVE Cheese is an important ingredient in many pasta dishes.

Parmesan/Parmigiano Reggiano Only the cheese made in the region of Reggio Emilia is allowed to be called Parmigiano Reggiano. Made from cows' milk it has a grainy texture with a fine, distinctive flavor. Best bought in chunks and grated when required. It can be bought in larger pieces, cut into smaller portions, then wrapped well and stored in the refrigerator. This way it will keep for months.

Romano A sheep milk cheese which has been aged for one year and is used mainly for grating. Has a sharper flavor than Parmesan.

Ricotta A soft cheese, similar to cottage cheese. Ideal as a binding agent and used in stuffings for filled pastas. It can be made from either cow, goat, or sheep milk. If watching your fat content, it is possible to buy a low-fat ricotta cheese, or you can substitute with cottage cheese.

Mozzarella Traditionally made from buffalo milk. Use grated or sliced on top of baked dishes, it can also be eaten raw. You can buy smoked and low fat mozzarella.

Fontina A semisoft cheese, used for cooking where a good melting cheese is required.

Mascarpone Similar to a thickened heavy whipping cream. Used traditionally in desserts such as Tiramisu or eaten as a table cheese with fresh fruit.

Dolcelatte A soft, mild, blue-veined cheese. The name means "sweet milk."

Gorgonzola A blue-greenish veined, soft, high-fat cheese from Lombardy. It has a sharp, pungent taste with a creamy texture. Often served at the end of a meal.

FISH

Tuna Used in several classic Italian dishes. As well as being canned in various oils, it is possible to buy tuna canned in spring water or brine if you are watching your calorie intake.

Anchovies The best anchovy fillets to buy are preserved in salt. Soak in water for 30 minutes and pat dry before use.

TOMATOES

Plum Tomatoes A good rich and full flavor, these should be used while still firm but ripe and red. The tomatoes grown in Italy are so full of flavor because they are ripened under the sun. As it is hard to reproduce this flavor, try using the alternatives listed below.

Sun-dried Tomatoes Available either in jars in oil or just dried in packages. Very concentrated, sweet flavor. Should be chopped and added to the sauce at the beginning of cooking.

Canned Tomatoes Available in various forms. The best alternative to fresh plum tomatoes.

Tomato Paste Sold in tubes, jars, or cans. An essential ingredient for many sauces for imparting an excellent tomato flavor.

Puréed Tomatoes Creamed or pulped tomatoes, sold in jars or cans.

HERBS, SPICES, AND SEASONINGS

Garlic An essential ingredient for most cuisines. Always choose firm, plump heads. It is now possible to obtain smoked garlic; however, if you cannot find it, ordinary garlic can be used in its place and the flavor of the recipe will not be impaired.

Capers Choose capers that are preserved in salt for a better flavor. Soak in water for 30 minutes before use.

Olives Black olives are the ones generally used but the green olives from Southern Italy are excellent.

Basil As well as the familiar green-leafed basil, opal basil is available, which is a beautiful purple color. Used extensively in salads as well as cooked dishes. Use at the end of cooking; tear or roughly chop before adding.

Flat Leaf or Continental Parsley Has a concentrated strong flavor, only worth using fresh.

Oregano A small leafed herb with a robust flavor.

Marjoram A spicy herb containing thymol in the leaves. Wild marjoram is also known as oregano, and grows wild in Italy and Greece.

Rosemary Aromatic, spiky needle-type leaves with a very distinctive flavor. Grows wild in Italy and the Mediterranean.

Sage Aromatic velvety leaves in varying colors from green, to gray, to purple. Widely used in Italy.

Nutmeg An aromatic seed with a strong, distinctive flavor, originating in Indonesia. Best used freshly grated.

Mushrooms

Dried Mushrooms These are normally wild mushrooms and have a very strong, meaty flavor, so use sparingly. They need reconstituting in water before use. Use the soaking liquor in sauces, having strained it first. Normally sold sliced. Once opened, keep in an airtight container to preserve the flavor. Porcini mushrooms are less expensive than morels. Morels have a very intense, bacon-like flavor and are dried whole. After soaking, they regain their original shape.

Wild Mushrooms Morels, chanterelles, and porcini are the most widely sold wild mushrooms. They all have a very distinctive flavor.

Cultivated Mushrooms Shiitake and oyster mushrooms are now widely cultivated and provide a welcome addition to the regular field or button mushrooms.

Truffles Perhaps one of the most expensive ingredients there is. Truffles cannot be cultivated and are "snuffed" out by pigs or dogs from under the ground. They are a fungi and available fresh from late fall through to winter. The white truffle from Alba, Piedmont, is the king of all. Its flavor is so intense that you only need a very small amount. It is normally just grated fresh over the finished dish, **never** used for cooking. The black truffle from Umbria or Perigord (France) does not have such an intense flavor and is used for cooking. You can sometimes obtain truffles that have been preserved in oil. If unable to obtain either black or white truffles, use truffle oil, which gives a hint of the flavor. Available from good delicatessens and food stores.

Chiles Obtainable either fresh or dried. The heat is contained not only in the seeds but also in their membranes. Take care when handling; if the chile juices get into your eyes, mouth, nose, or an open wound, it smarts immensely. Wash hands thoroughly after use. Different chiles have different heat levels. As a general rule, the smaller the chile, the higher the heat level. If in doubt, use a variety sparingly until you know its heat level. Dried chiles tend to be hot.

WINE NOTES

Wine must complement the food with which it is served. There are many to choose from, from all over the world. Whether you choose New World wines from California, Australia, New Zealand, and South Africa, or you choose the more classic varieties from France, Italy, and Spain, the same rules apply. The choice of wine depends not only on your personal palate but also on the food served and how it has been prepared. However, rules are continuously being broken and it is always a good idea to try a wide variety of the many wines that are so readily available.

Wines made from the same grape vary from region to region and from year to year. The amount of sun, the soil, and the climate also play a critical part in the flavor and bouquet of the wine produced. Each producer combines different grapes and employs various methods in the production of their wines. There are so many excellent wines to choose from it would be a shame if you drank the same wines year after year.

With vinegary, citrus-based dishes or very strong spicy dishes, such as curries or chili, it is pointless to serve a light, delicate wine or a robust wine; the acidity or spicy hot flavor of the dish will completely destroy the aroma and bouquet of the wine. It is better to serve chilled beer or lager or even a chilled mineral water in anticipation of the wines to come.

For pasta dishes that consist of fish, shellfish, or vegetables, the type of wine to choose is the one that you would normally serve with fish or vegetables. Try well-chilled white wines with a good fresh tangy acidity and plenty of flavor such as Pouilly Fumé from France, or one of the New World wines such as Delegat's Hawkes Bay Sauvignon Blanc from New Zealand or Columbia Crest Sauvignon Blanc from Washington State.

Dishes that incorporate chicken are best served with either a full-flavored white wine such as Cooks Chardonnay from New Zealand or a Chablis from France. You could also try a lighter red, such as Chianti Classico from Italy or Mountain View Pinot Noir from California.

Pastas with a meat sauce need strong robust wines, so a Tollana Cabernet-Shiraz from southern Australia or Merlot Collio from Italy would be ideal.

With any of the pastas that contain game, the general rule is that the stronger the flavor of the food, the more robust the wine required. A Burgundy such as Gevrey Chambertin from France would be ideal, as would Barolo from Italy or Jensen Vineyard Pinot Noir from California.

CHAPTER TWO

HOMEMADE PASTA

In this chapter you will find information and tips on making your own pasta, with some interesting and innovative new ideas for you to try when you have become proficient at pasta making. Easy-to-follow, step-by-step guides to using your pasta machine take the mystique out of the whole process.

BASIC PASTA DOUGH

The recipe below is ideal when making the dough by hand and using a pasta machine that rolls and cuts out basic shapes. However, some electrically operated machines and hand-operated extruders make the pasta as well. In this case, do check the manufacturer's instructions before using your machine for the first time. Plus, of course, there are some safety precautions when using an electrically operated machine that are critical (see page 9).

When making homemade pasta, ensure that the eggs are at room temperature and do not knead the dough on a very cold surface. Pasta dough needs to be kept warm while it is being made.

Makes 1 lb pasta dough

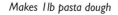

- 2½ cups durum wheat flour (or Italian "OO" flour) or all-purpose flour
- pinch of sea salt
- 3 medium eggs
- 1 tbsp virgin olive oil

   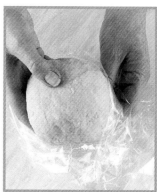

1 Place the flour and salt in a mound on a clean work surface or in a large bowl. Make a well in the center. Break the eggs one by one into the center of the well and beat with a fork until the eggs are evenly mixed together. Add the oil to the eggs.

2 Gradually incorporate the flour from inside the well into the egg until the egg is no longer runny. Take care not to break the wall of flour or the egg will escape. Using both hands, quickly bring the flour up over the egg mixture. Work until all the flour is mixed into the egg. Mix to form a stiff dough, adding a little water if necessary.

3 The dough should feel moist but not sticky. Wrap in plastic wrap if not rolling immediately. Clean your hands and, if necessary, the work surface. Hold the dough with one hand and fold it over with the fingers of the other hand. Knead the dough with the heel of your palm, rotating the dough a quarter of a turn.

4 Knead by pushing the dough down and away from you. Continue kneading the dough until it feels very smooth. It is better to make the dough in small batches (1 lb) for easier handling. Wrap in plastic wrap and let rest 20 minutes before rolling out and using.

To make wholewheat pasta, substitute the white flour with wholewheat strong flour. If you wish, you can use half durum wheat flour and half wholewheat flour. You may need a little extra oil to make a soft and pliable dough.

COLORED AND FLAVORED PASTA DOUGH

As well as being made in all kinds of shapes and sizes, pasta can also be made in a variety of different colors and flavors. Colored, flavored pastas provide an interesting and delicious change, and are easily achieved.

SPINACH PASTA (PASTA VERDI)

Wash 8oz fresh spinach thoroughly, discarding the tough stems and outer leaves. Place in a large pan with just the water that is left clinging to the leaves and cook for 3 minutes or until tender. Drain thoroughly, squeeze out as much moisture as possible using paper towels, then chop very finely. Add to the eggs before the flour is mixed into the basic pasta dough. You may need to add a little extra flour to the pasta to absorb any excess moisture.

SAFFRON PASTA

Infuse 1 teaspoon saffron strands in 1 teaspoon warm water for 15 minutes. Add to the eggs before the flour is mixed into the basic pasta dough.

TOMATO PASTA

Add 2–3 tablespoons tomato paste to the eggs before the flour is mixed into the basic pasta dough.

BLACK PASTA

Add 1 teaspoon squid ink to the eggs before the flour is mixed into the basic pasta dough. Take care not to use too much excess flour when making this pasta or the density of the color will be lost.

MUSHROOM PASTA

Reconstitute 1oz dried porcini in 3 tablespoons boiling water for at least 30 minutes. Thoroughly drain, squeezing out excess moisture with paper towels, and chop very finely. Add to the eggs before the flour is mixed into the basic pasta dough.

BEET PASTA

Purée 1oz fresh cooked beet and rub through a sieve to remove any lumps. Add to the eggs before the flour is mixed into the basic pasta dough. For a darker colored pasta, use an extra 1oz sieved beet.

HERB PASTA

Finely chop 3 tablespoons fresh herbs and mix into the eggs before the flour is mixed into the basic pasta dough. Try basil, oregano, sage, tarragon, mint, or even a combination of two or three different herbs. For added flavor, add 1–2 minced garlic cloves, 1 seeded and finely chopped chile, or 1 tablespoon grated lemon rind.

CHOCOLATE PASTA

Melt 2oz semisweet chocolate or very good dark chocolate in a bowl placed over a pan of gently simmering water, or use the microwave. Cool slightly and mix into the eggs. Add 2 tablespoons sifted unsweetened cocoa powder to the flour. Mix the melted chocolate into the basic pasta dough when the eggs are being added.

CITRUS PASTA

Add 2 tablespoons freshly grated lemon, lime, or orange rind, or a mixture of all three rinds to the eggs before the flour is mixed into the basic pasta dough.

HOW TO USE YOUR ROLLING AND CUTTING MACHINE

1 Clamp your machine securely onto the work surface and insert the handle. Turn the regulator knob so that it is at its widest setting. Wipe the machine thoroughly with a clean cloth (see also page 8).

2 Cut the prepared dough in half, flour lightly, and feed each half through the rollers while turning the handle.

3 Sprinkle with a very light dusting of flour and fold in half. Press the seams together firmly with the heel of your hand.

4 Pass through the roller a further six to eight times, until the dough feels smooth and elastic, folding the dough in half and lightly dusting with flour after each time.

5 Decrease space between the rollers one notch at a time. Feed the dough through without folding in half. If it becomes unmanageable, cut it in half and cover one half with a dish towel while rolling the other half.

6 Lightly dust the dough with flour to prevent it sticking to the rollers. When the dough has reached the right thickness, cover with a clean dish towel and let dry about 5–10 minutes before cutting.

CUTTING THE DOUGH

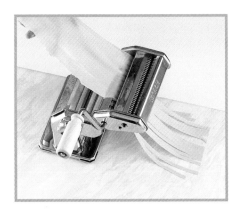 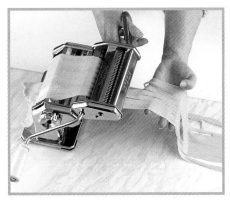 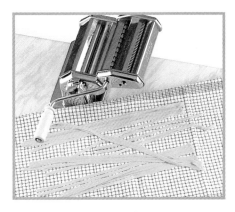

1 Attach the cutting head to the machine by sliding the attachments into the brackets on either side of the machine. Before you cut the pasta, it must feel dry so that the pasta does not stick to itself. Take care not to let it become too dry or brittle, however, as then it will not cut properly. Carefully pass the pasta through the cutting head, turning the handle at the same time.

2 When the cut pasta has reached the correct length, cut with a pair of scissors. Toss with a little flour.

3 If you are cooking the pasta within 1 hour, place flat on a clean dish towel. If you are keeping the pasta for longer, whether a few hours or days, wrap loosely round your hand to form small nests and place on a dish towel to dry. Store in an airtight jar.

MAKING RAVIOLI

Ravioli is easy to make when using your pasta machine. The ravioli attachment cuts three rows of mini filled cases of pasta. It can be stuffed with a variety of fillings, such as ricotta cheese, spinach, or ham.

1 Prepare the dough as before and roll it until a long, thin sheet of pasta is achieved. Cut the sheet of pasta with the cutter enclosed with the ravioli attachment and dust with flour. Clamp the machine to the table and fix the ravioli attachment to the machine. Fold the sheet of pasta dough in half and insert the closed half into the plastic hopper of the ravioli attachment.

NOTE If you do not have the ravioli attachment for your machine, simply roll out the pasta dough as thinly as possible. Cut out 2–3 inch squares or rounds with a pastry cutter. Place a small spoonful of the filling in the center; dampen the edges, and fold over to encase the filling. Pinch the edges very firmly together. Let dry at least 1 hour on a floured plate.

2 Carefully separate the pasta and lay each sheet over the wooden roller of the hopper. Turn the handle slowly until the pasta has been caught by the rollers and the two pasta sheets sealed together.

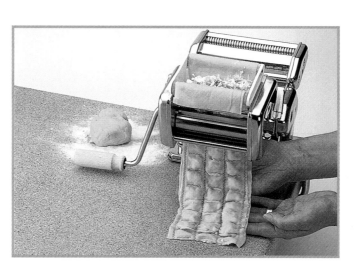

3 Prepare the stuffing and use to fill the hopper. Turn the handle slowly and three rows of filled cases will begin to appear. Repeat, filling the hopper with any remaining stuffing. Sprinkle with a little flour and let the ravioli dry 1 hour before cutting.

USING A HAND-OPERATED EXTRUDER PASTA MACHINE

Different makes of machine vary so it is always advisable to check before buying your machine to ensure that it will give you the pasta you require.

Ensure you clean the machine well after use. Turn the handle in the opposite direction and remove the hopper. Loosen the closing ring nut with the wrench and remove the fork and cutter or die holder. Turn the chamber counterclockwise to remove the extruder parts. Completely remove all the pieces of the machine that are removable, wash in hot soapy water, dry well, and reassemble after a few hours when the parts are completely dry. Any remaining pieces of pasta can be removed with a clean, dry brush.

Never wash your machine parts in a dishwasher.

1 Wipe the machine with a clean cloth. Clamp the machine securely to the work surface with the clamp provided and insert the handle in the SLOW opening. (The fast opening is used only for meat mincing and dough making.) Fit the die of the shape you wish to extrude.

Make the dough and leave to relax, wrapped in plastic wrap. Place a small piece of dough into the hopper and slowly turn the handle.

2 After a few seconds the shapes will begin to come out of the die in the machine. When they have reached the required length, cut with a sharp knife. Repeat until all the pasta has been cut. If the pasta shapes are sticking together, sprinkle with a little flour. Leave to dry for about 1 hour before cooking.

3 To change the die, turn the turning handle a few times in the opposite direction and lift up and remove the hopper. Using the wrench, unscrew the closing ring nut. Choose the cutter or die you wish to use and place on the end of the extrusion barrel. Ensure that it fits correctly with the four tabs of the die engaged in the notches on the barrel. Screw the ring nut back, put the hopper back in place, and begin to extrude your pasta.

MAKING PASTA SHAPES

If you do not have a machine which produces shaped pastas, or you want a pasta shape that cannot be made from a machine, below are instructions as to how you can make some of the most popular shapes by hand.

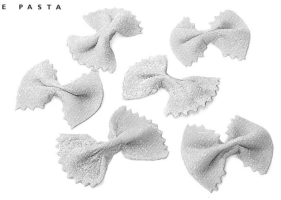

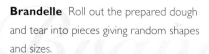

Brandelle Roll out the prepared dough and tear into pieces giving random shapes and sizes.

Garganelli Cut a 2-inch square of pasta, moisten one side with water, then roll at an angle around the handle of a wooden spoon. Allow to dry then remove from handle.

Farfalle Roll your prepared dough into a rectangle and divide into neat 2-inch squares. Using a serrated pastry cutter or wheel, divide the squares in half. Pinch the center of each halved square to form a bow or butterfly shape.

Fusilli Cut 2-inch squares of pasta into four strips. Roll around a thick skewer to form a spiral. Lightly roll over a grooved wooden butter shaper, remove, and allow to dry.

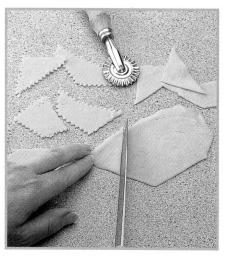

Maltagliati Roll out the pasta dough into a rectangle then cut out irregular shapes using a sharp knife or a plain or serrated pastry cutter.

Orecchiette Roll small pieces of dough into balls about ½–1-inch diameter. Press in the center of each ball, allowing the pasta to curl upwards so there is a hollow in the center.

COOKING AND SERVING PASTA

It is important for the greatest enjoyment of pasta that it is cooked correctly. "Al dente" is the classic Italian expression used to describe the texture of pasta when it is correctly cooked. It should still be slightly firm with a bite to it. The only way to check is by tasting. Simply remove a piece of the pasta from the saucepan and bite it; if it has a chewy feel, then it is ready. Fresh pasta such as angel hair can take as little as 30 seconds to cook; by the time the water has come back to a boil after the pasta has been added, it is virtually ready. Other fresh pasta can take 1–2 minutes, while lasagna sheets can take 3–4 minutes.

To test if filled pastas are cooked, taste the edge of the pasta rather than trying to cut through the stuffing.

Dried pasta takes longer to cook; again the best way to check is by tasting.

As a general rule, allow 7 pints water to 1 lb pasta. Use a large saucepan which will enable the pasta to move around in the water. Bring the water to a boil before adding any salt or the pasta. Use 1 tablespoon salt for 1 lb pasta. Add the salt as the water comes to a boil, then add the pasta all at once.

NOTE It is a misconception that oil needs to be added to the water when cooking pasta. Cooking the pasta in plenty of water and stirring frequently just after the pasta has been added should prevent most pastas from sticking together. The only exception is when cooking the large, flat ribbon pastas, such as lasagna.

Immediately after the pasta has been added, stir to prevent it sticking to the pan. This will also help to submerge long strands of pasta. Put a lid on the pan to bring the water back to a boil as quickly as possible. Once the water has come back to a boil, remove the lid. Stir occasionally and taste until the pasta is cooked to "al dente."

Drain immediately through a colander and shake gently. Always save a little of the pasta cooking water; it is ideal for thinning down sauces if they are too thick. Do not rinse as this cools the pasta and removes the starch which makes the sauce stick to the pasta.

As a general rule, if serving pasta as an appetizer, allow 3–4oz of fresh pasta per person. If it is served as a main meal with meat, fish, or vegetables in a sauce with a green salad, allow 4–5oz of fresh pasta per serving.

The recipes serve six as appetizers and four when served as a main meal with a green salad and crusty bread. The desserts serve four.

NUTRITIONAL ANALYSIS

The analysis has been based upon each meal serving four people and it takes into account only the pasta dish itself and not any accompaniments that you may choose to serve with the meal.

The top panel of the data box provides information required to know the portion size and a nutritional analysis based upon one serving. The bottom panel details information about the Daily Values based upon a 2,000 calorie a day diet, the current public health recommendation for older adults, sedentary women, and children. An active man, teenage boys, and very active women need a higher calorie intake than a sedentary adult.

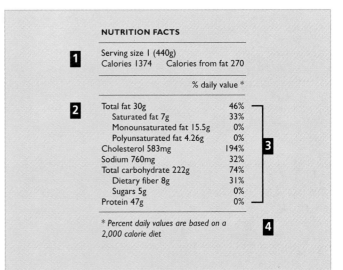

NUTRITION FACTS

1 Serving size 1 (440g)
Calories 1374   Calories from fat 270

                                          % daily value *

2
	% daily value *
Total fat 30g	46%
Saturated fat 7g	33%
Monounsaturated fat 15.5g	0%
Polyunsaturated fat 4.26g	0%
Cholesterol 583mg	194%
Sodium 760mg	32%
Total carbohydrate 222g	74%
Dietary fiber 8g	31%
Sugars 5g	0%
Protein 47g	0%

3

* Percent daily values are based on a 2,000 calorie diet

4

1 Serving size for one portion, in metric measure. Since the serving size is defined, it is easier to make a meaningful comparison of nutritional benefits.

2 Nutrients most important to health today.

3 % daily value indicates how intake fits into overall daily diet. Use this information to quickly determine if the dish is high or low in a nutrient.

4 A reference value based on a person's calorie need. An active teenager will need a higher daily calorie intake than a sedentary adult.

Source: Food Labeling Education Information Center, FDA/USDA.

CHAPTER THREE

CLASSIC SAUCES

Sauces play an integral part in the eating of pasta. A good sauce can often mean the difference between an indifferent meal and one of true gastronomic delight. The sauces in this chapter are those that are the most popular and traditional to serve with pasta. They can also be used in baked or filled pasta dishes.

SPICY TOMATO SAUCE

This sauce is made hot and spicy by the use of fresh jalapeño chiles. Dried crushed chiles can be substituted; use ¼–½ teaspoon depending on how hot you like it.

Makes 1 pint

For the sauce

◆ 1½ lb fresh plum tomatoes
◆ 3 tbsp virgin olive oil
◆ 1-2 garlic cloves, peeled and minced
◆ 1-2 jalapeño chiles, seeded and finely chopped
◆ 2 tbsp tomato paste
◆ 1 tbsp roughly chopped fresh oregano
◆ salt and ground black pepper

To serve

◆ 1lb fresh pasta
◆ freshly grated Romano cheese

Make a small cross in the top of each tomato and place in a large bowl. Cover with boiling water and leave for 2-3 minutes. Drain and peel. Cut into quarters, discard the seeds, then roughly chop the flesh.

Heat the oil in a pan and gently sauté the garlic and chiles for 3 minutes, taking care not to let the garlic or chiles burn. Add the chopped tomatoes and tomato paste blended with 2 tablespoons water. Bring to a boil, reduce the heat, and simmer for 15 minutes or until a sauce consistency is reached. Add the chopped oregano with seasoning to taste and let simmer while you cook the pasta.

Cook the pasta in plenty of salted boiling water for 1-2 minutes or until "al dente." Drain and toss with the sauce. Serve immediately, handing the grated cheese separately.

NUTRITION FACTS

Serving size 1 (319g)
Calories 523   Calories from fat 189

	% daily value *
Total fat 21g	33%
Saturated fat 5g	25%
Monounsaturated fat 12.3g	0%
Polyunsaturated fat 2.2g	0%
Cholesterol 157mg	52%
Sodium 572mg	24%
Total carbohydrate 66g	22%
Dietary fiber 4g	18%
Sugars 7g	0%
Protein 17g	0%

* Percent daily values are based on a 2,000-calorie diet

Pesto

Perhaps one of the best-loved and well-known of all the sauces, now used in many other dishes as well as pasta. Originating in the Liguria region of Italy, where the Genoese grow the tiny sweet basil leaves to make their world-famous pesto.

Makes 1 cup

NUTRITION FACTS

Serving size 1 (178g)
Calories 704   Calories from fat 396

	% daily value *
Total fat 44g	68%
Saturated fat 9g	44%
Monounsaturated fat 26.9g	0%
Polyunsaturated fat 5.1g	0%
Cholesterol 158mg	53%
Sodium 589mg	25%
Total carbohydrate 59g	20%
Dietary fiber 2g	10%
Sugars 1g	0%
Protein 20g	0%

* *Percent daily values are based on a 2,000-calorie diet*

For the sauce
◆ 2oz fresh basil leaves
◆ 8 tbsp extra virgin olive oil
◆ ¼ cup pine nuts
◆ 2-3 garlic cloves, peeled
◆ salt
◆ ½ cup freshly grated Parmesan cheese
◆ 1 tbsp freshly grated Romano cheese

To serve
◆ 1lb fresh pasta
◆ extra freshly grated Parmesan cheese
◆ fresh basil leaves

Place the fresh basil leaves, extra virgin olive oil, pine nuts, and garlic in a food processor and blend the ingredients together until smooth. Spoon into a bowl and stir in salt to taste and the freshly grated cheeses.

Meanwhile, cook the pasta in plenty of salted boiling water for 1-2 minutes or until "al dente." Drain and toss with the pesto sauce. Serve immediately with extra freshly grated cheese and a few basil leaves to garnish.

CARBONARA

There are many different variations of this sauce, but they all use the same basic ingredients, although the proportions may vary. For those seeking a slightly healthier version of this classic sauce, omit the butter and increase the oil by 2 tablespoons, then substitute thick yogurt for the cream.

Makes 1 cup

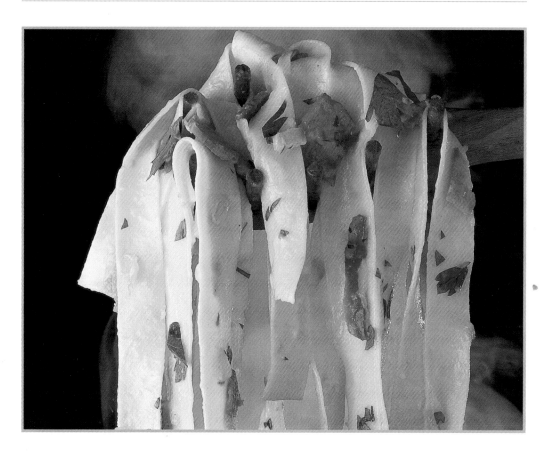

NUTRITION FACTS

Serving size 1 (215g)
Calories 830   Calories from fat 486

	% daily value *
Total fat 54g	84%
Saturated fat 22g	108%
Monounsaturated fat 24.9g	0%
Polyunsaturated fat 4.5g	0%
Cholesterol 330mg	110%
Sodium 1009mg	42%
Total carbohydrate 58g	19%
Dietary fiber 2g	8%
Sugars 2g	0%
Protein 26g	0%

* Percent daily values are based on a 2,000-calorie diet

For the sauce
- 2 tbsp unsalted butter
- 3 tbsp olive oil
- 2-3 garlic cloves, peeled and minced
- 1 large onion, peeled and finely chopped
- 4oz pancetta or smoked lean bacon slices, cut into thin strips
- 2 medium egg yolks
- ⅔ cup light whipping cream
- 4 tbsp freshly grated Parmesan cheese
- salt and ground black pepper

To serve
- 1lb fresh pasta
- 2 tbsp freshly grated Parmesan cheese
- chopped fresh flat leaf parsley

Heat the unsalted butter and oil in a pan and gently sauté the garlic and onion for 5 minutes or until softened but not browned. Add the pancetta or smoked bacon and continue to sauté for 2 more minutes.

Beat the egg yolks with the cream and 4 tablespoons of Parmesan, reserve.

Meanwhile, cook the pasta in plenty of salted boiling water for 1-2 minutes or until "al dente."

Drain thoroughly and return to the pan. Add the onion and pancetta mixture and heat through for 2 minutes stirring occasionally, then remove from the heat.

Add the egg and cream mixture and quickly mix together with two forks so that the eggs are cooked in the heat of the pasta. Season to taste and serve immediately with the Parmesan and sprinkle with chopped parsley.

FRESH TOMATO SAUCE

When making tomato sauce, look for tomatoes that are properly ripened but not over-ripe. For a true authentic taste, use plum tomatoes.

Makes 2½ cups

NUTRITION FACTS

Serving size 1 (396g)
Calories 497   Calories from fat 171

	% daily value *
Total fat 19g	29%
Saturated fat 3g	15%
Monounsaturated fat 11.4g	0%
Polyunsaturated fat 2.1g	0%
Cholesterol 146mg	49%
Sodium 693mg	29%
Total carbohydrate 68g	23%
Dietary fiber 5g	18%
Sugars 8g	0%
Protein 15g	0%

* Percent daily values are based on a 2,000-calorie diet

For the sauce
- 1½ lb tomatoes
- ½ small fennel bulb (about 2 tbsp chopped)
- 3 tbsp olive oil
- 1 onion, peeled and chopped
- 2-3 garlic cloves, peeled and minced
- few sprigs of oregano
- 2-3 tbsp tomato paste
- 1¼ cups vegetable stock
- salt and ground black pepper

To serve
- 1lb fresh pasta
- 1-2 tsp chopped fresh oregano

Make a small cross in the top of each tomato and place in a large bowl. Cover with boiling water and leave for 2 minutes. Drain off the water and peel the tomatoes. Cut in half and chop roughly. Trim the fennel, discarding any damaged outer leaves, then chop finely.

Heat the oil in a pan and gently sauté the fennel, onion, and garlic for 5 minutes or until soft but not browned. Add the chopped tomatoes with the oregano sprigs and continue to sauté for 3 more minutes.

Blend the tomato paste with a little of the vegetable stock, then add to the pan with the remaining stock. Bring to a boil and simmer for 10-12 minutes or until reduced to a sauce consistency. Remove the oregano sprigs and add seasoning to taste.

Meanwhile, cook the pasta in plenty of salted boiling water for 1-2 minutes or until "al dente." Drain the pasta thoroughly and add to the sauce with the chopped oregano. Toss lightly, then serve immediately.

CLAM AND CHILE SAUCE

When cooking clams the same rule applies to clams as to mussels. Discard those that are open before cooking and those that remain closed after cooking.

Makes 2 cups

For the sauce
- 2 lb fresh clams
- 4 tbsp olive oil
- 1 garlic clove, peeled and minced
- 2 shallots, peeled and chopped
- 1 jalapeño chile, seeded and finely chopped
- 1¼ cups dry white wine
- salt and ground black pepper
- 4 tbsp light whipping cream (optional)

To serve
- 1 lb fresh pasta
- 2 tbsp chopped fresh flat parsley

Scrub the clam shells and soak in cold water at least 30 minutes, discarding any that remain open. (If you tap an open clam before cooking and it closes, you can use it.) Drain the clams just before using.

Heat the oil in a large pan and gently sauté the garlic, shallots, and chile for 5 minutes or until softened. Add the wine and simmer gently for 5 minutes.

Add the drained clams, cover with a lid, and steam for 5 minutes or until all the clams have opened. Carefully shake the pan occasionally until the clams have opened. Discard any that remain closed. Remove from the heat and stir in the seasoning and cream.

Meanwhile, cook the pasta in plenty of salted boiling water for 1-2 minutes or until cooked to almost "al dente." Drain the pasta thoroughly and reserve.

Add the pasta to the clam pan and place over a medium heat. Continue to cook for 1-2 minutes or until the pasta has finished cooking. Remove from the heat and add the parsley. Stir and serve immediately.

NUTRITION FACTS

Serving size 1 (447g)
Calories 727   Calories from fat 252

	% daily value *
Total fat 28g	43%
Saturated fat 7g	33%
Monounsaturated fat 15.4g	0%
Polyunsaturated fat 2.9g	0%
Cholesterol 238mg	79%
Sodium 544mg	23%
Total carbohydrate 63g	21%
Dietary fiber 2g	9%
Sugars 2g	0%
Protein 41g	0%

* Percent daily values are based on a 2,000-calorie diet

SPRING VEGETABLE AND CREAM SAUCE

You can generally buy most vegetables all year round. However, when home-grown produce first comes into the stores or the new baby vegetables first appear, make the most of them and make this delicious sauce.

Makes 2 cups

For the sauce
- 3oz young asparagus, trimmed
- 3oz new or baby carrots, trimmed
- ½ cup shelled fava beans
- ½ cup snow peas
- 4 tbsp unsalted butter
- 2 shallots, peeled and chopped
- ¾ cup diced zucchini

- scant 1 cup heavy whipping cream
- salt and ground black pepper
- 4 tbsp freshly grated Parmigiano Reggiano cheese

To serve
- 1lb fresh pasta
- sprig of opal basil

Cut the asparagus into short lengths. Blanch in lightly salted boiling water for 2 minutes. Drain and refresh in cold water, then drain again.

Slice long carrots or cut baby carrots in half. Cook in lightly salted boiling water for 2-3 minutes or until almost tender. Drain and refresh in cold water, then drain again. Blanch the fava beans for 3 minutes and the snow peas for 1 minute. Refresh in cold water and drain.

Melt the unsalted butter in a large pan and gently sauté the shallots for 5 minutes. Add the zucchini and sauté for a further 1 minute. Add all the drained, refreshed vegetables to the heavy whipping cream and cook gently, stirring, for about 5-8 minutes or until the cream has reduced slightly.

Meanwhile, cook the pasta in plenty of salted boiling water for 1-2 minutes or until "al dente." Drain thoroughly, then add to the vegetable and cream sauce. Add seasoning to taste with the grated cheese. Heat through gently for 1 minute. Garnish with a sprig of opal basil.

SUN-DRIED TOMATO AND BLACK OLIVE SAUCE

This is a robust sauce and is ideally suited to the thicker ribbons of pasta, such as tagliatelle, or shapes such as penne or garganelli.

Makes 1 cup

NUTRITION FACTS

Serving size 1 (272g)
Calories 590   Calories from fat 216

	% daily value *
Total fat 24g	37%
Saturated fat 6g	28%
Monounsaturated fat 12.4g	0%
Polyunsaturated fat 2.5g	0%
Cholesterol 160mg	53%
Sodium 1082mg	45%
Total carbohydrate 74g	25%
Dietary fiber 4g	16%
Sugars 3g	0%
Protein 21g	0%

* Percent daily values are based on a 2,000-calorie diet

For the sauce
- 2 tbsp olive oil
- 8 sun-dried tomatoes in oil, finely chopped
- 1 tbsp sun-dried tomato oil
- 1 medium onion, peeled and finely chopped
- 2 garlic cloves, peeled and minced
- 2 celery stems, trimmed and finely chopped
- 2oz pancetta, chopped
- ½ cup pitted and chopped black olives
- 1 tbsp tomato paste
- 1¼ cups vegetable stock
- few sprigs of marjoram
- salt and ground black pepper

To serve
- 1lb fresh pasta
- extra sprigs marjoram
- freshly grated Parmesan cheese

Heat the olive oil and 1 tablespoon of sun-dried tomato oil in a pan and sauté the onion, sun-dried tomatoes, garlic, celery, and pancetta for 5 minutes. Stir in half the olives.

Blend the tomato paste with a little of the stock, then stir into the pan with the remaining stock and the marjoram. Bring to a boil and simmer for 10 minutes. Cool, then pass through a food processor and return to the pan. Add seasoning to taste with the remaining olives. Cover with a lid and remove from the heat.

Meanwhile, cook the pasta in plenty of salted boiling water for 1-2 minutes or until "al dente." Drain well, then add the tomato sauce and toss lightly. Serve immediately, scattered with roughly torn marjoram sprigs and Parmesan.

QUICK TOMATO SAUCE

This sauce is ideal when time is critical and you are relying on store cupboard ingredients. It is also an excellent sauce to use for filled pasta as well as layered dishes.

Makes I cup

NUTRITION FACTS

Serving size 1 (222g)

Calories 430	Calories from fat 135

	% daily value *
Total fat 15g	23%
Saturated fat 3g	14%
Monounsaturated fat 8.9g	0%
Polyunsaturated fat 1.6g	0%
Cholesterol 147mg	49%
Sodium 619mg	26%
Total carbohydrate 59g	20%
Dietary fiber 3g	12%
Sugars 1g	0%
Protein 14g	0%

* Percent daily values are based on a 2,000-calorie diet

For the sauce
- 2 tbsp olive oil
- 1 large onion, peeled and grated
- 14oz can chopped tomatoes
- salt and ground black pepper
- few dashes hot pepper sauce

To serve
- 1lb fresh pasta
- freshly shaved Parmesan cheese

Heat the oil in a large pan and sauté the onion for 5 minutes. Add the contents of the can of tomatoes and sauté gently for 10 minutes. Add seasoning and hot pepper sauce to taste, cover with a lid and remove from the heat.

Meanwhile, cook the pasta in plenty of boiling water for 1-2 minutes or until "al dente." Drain thoroughly, then return to the pan. Add the tomato sauce to the cooked pasta. Heat through for 2 minutes, tossing lightly, then serve immediately, sprinkled with fresh shavings of Parmesan cheese.

GARLIC AND OLIVE OIL SAUCE

One of the simplest of sauces yet one of the most delicious. As with good wines, the better the olive oil used the better the taste, so don't skimp on the quality of the oil.

Makes ⅔ cup

NUTRITION FACTS

Serving size 1 (137g)
Calories 556   Calories from fat 279

	% daily value *
Total fat 31g	48%
Saturated fat 5g	24%
Monounsaturated fat 21.3g	0%
Polyunsaturated fat 3.1g	0%
Cholesterol 146mg	49%
Sodium 336mg	14%
Total carbohydrate 56g	19%
Dietary fiber 2g	8%
Sugars 1g	0%
Protein 12g	0%

* Percent daily values are based on a 2,000-calorie diet

For the sauce
◆ 2-4 garlic cloves, peeled
◆ 6-8 tbsp extra virgin olive oil
◆ salt and ground black pepper
◆ 1 tbsp roughly chopped fresh flat leaf parsley

To serve
◆ 1lb fresh pasta

Finely chop the garlic. Place in a pan with the oil and sauté gently for 5 minutes. Add seasoning to taste with the parsley, cover the pan with a lid, and remove from the heat.

Meanwhile, cook the pasta in plenty of salted boiling water for 1-2 minutes or until "al dente." Drain and add the garlic sauce. Toss lightly, then serve immediately.

Ragu

This sauce is native to the Italian city of Bologna. There, every family has its own recipe, which has been passed down through the generations.

Makes 2 cups

NUTRITION FACTS

Serving size 1 (416g)
Calories 716   Calories from fat 297

	% daily value *
Total fat 33g	50%
Saturated fat 10g	49%
Monounsaturated fat 16.6g	0%
Polyunsaturated fat 2.4g	0%
Cholesterol 211mg	70%
Sodium 686mg	29%
Total carbohydrate 64g	21%
Dietary fiber 4g	17%
Sugars 4g	0%
Protein 30g	0%

* Percent daily values are based on a 2,000-calorie diet

For the sauce
- 2 tbsp olive oil
- 2-4 garlic cloves, peeled and minced
- 1 onion, peeled and finely chopped
- 2 celery stems, trimmed and finely chopped
- 1 large carrot, peeled and diced
- 12oz lean ground beef
- 1 cup dry white wine
- 14oz can chopped tomatoes
- 1 tbsp tomato paste
- salt and ground black pepper
- 1 tbsp chopped fresh oregano

To serve
- 1lb fresh pasta
- freshly grated Parmesan cheese

Heat the olive oil in a large pan and sauté the garlic, onion, celery stems, and diced carrot for 5-8 minutes or until softened but not browned. Add the beef and continue to sauté for 5 minutes or until sealed, stirring frequently to break up any lumps.

Add the wine and the contents of the can of tomatoes. Blend the tomato paste with 2 tablespoons water and stir into the pan. Bring to a boil, cover with a lid, then simmer for 20 minutes or until a thick consistency is reached. Add seasoning to taste with the chopped oregano, cover with a lid, and remove from the heat. Reserve.

Meanwhile, cook the pasta in plenty of boiling salted water for 1-2 minutes or until "al dente." Drain thoroughly and return to the pan. Add the sauce and toss lightly. Either stir in the grated Parmesan cheese or pass the cheese separately. Serve immediately.

BUTTER AND TOMATO SAUCE

Always use unsalted butter when cooking, as it imparts a far better flavor.
You can also control the salt content far better.

Makes 2 cups

For the sauce

- 1½ lb ripe beefsteak tomatoes, peeled
- 6 tbsp unsalted butter
- 6 shallots, peeled and finely chopped
- 3 tbsp fresh basil leaves
- salt and ground black pepper

To serve

- 1lb fresh pasta
- basil leaves
- freshly grated Parmigiano Reggiano cheese

Seed and dice the tomatoes. Melt 4 tablespoons of butter in a large pan and gently sauté for 5 minutes or until softened but not browned. Add the remaining butter and the tomatoes and continue to sauté gently for 5-8 minutes or until the tomatoes have begun to break down. Stir in the basil leaves with seasoning to taste. Cover with a lid and remove from the heat.

Meanwhile, cook the pasta in plenty of salted boiling water for 1-2 minutes or until "al dente." Drain thoroughly and add to the tomato sauce. Toss lightly and serve immediately, garnished with extra basil leaves. Hand some freshly grated Parmigiano Reggiano cheese separately.

NUTRITION FACTS

Serving size 1 (307g)
Calories 553   Calories from fat 243

	% daily value *
Total fat 27g	42%
Saturated fat 14g	68%
Monounsaturated fat 9.4g	0%
Polyunsaturated fat 1.9g	0%
Cholesterol 197mg	66%
Sodium 438mg	18%
Total carbohydrate 64g	21%
Dietary fiber 4g	15%
Sugars 6g	0%
Protein 14g	0%

* Percent daily values are based on a 2,000-calorie diet

CHAPTER FOUR

PASTA SHAPES

It is very easy to make all kinds of shapes with the pasta that you have made using your machine. Just turn to the front of the book to see how to cut them once you have made the basic dough. Some pasta shapes are better suited to certain dishes than others, so think about the sauce you are serving.

GARGANELLI WITH CHICKEN

I am a great lover of dried apricots and the addition of apricots here gives this dish an added dimension.

For the sauce
- 8oz boneless, skinless chicken breast meat
- 4 tbsp olive oil
- 2 garlic cloves, peeled and cut into thin slivers
- 1 red onion, peeled and sliced into thin wedges
- 1 orange bell pepper, seeded and thinly sliced
- ½ cup chopped ready-to-eat dried apricots

- 1 tbsp chopped fresh rosemary
- 4 tbsp dry white wine
- salt and ground black pepper

To serve
- 1lb fresh garganelli
- freshly shaved Romano cheese

Discard any sinews from the chicken and cut into thin strips. Heat the oil in a skillet and sauté the garlic and onion for 5 minutes or until softened. Add the chicken and continue to sauté, stirring, for 3 minutes, or until the chicken is completely sealed.

Add the pepper, apricots, and rosemary and cook for 1 minute, then add the wine with seasoning to taste. Bring to a boil, cover with a and simmer for 3-4 minutes or until the chicken is cooked. Remove from the heat.

Meanwhile, cook the garganelli in plenty of boiling salted water for 1-2 minutes or until "al dente." Drain, reserving 2 tablespoons of the pasta cooking liquor. Return the pasta and liquor to the pan with the cooked chicken mixture and toss lightly. Serve immediately with the freshly shaved cheese.

NUTRITION FACTS

Serving size 1 (301g)
Calories 719   Calories from fat 279

	% daily value *
Total fat 31g	48%
Saturated fat 5g	27%
Monounsaturated fat 16.13g	0%
Polyunsaturated fat 3.18g	0%
Cholesterol 177mg	59%
Sodium 593mg	25%
Total carbohydrate 78g	26%
Dietary fiber 5g	19%
Sugars 9g	0%
Protein 30g	0%

* Percent daily values are based on a 2,000-calorie diet

MALTAGLIATI WITH PORCINI

Fresh porcini are very hard to find especially outside of Italy. Look for dried porcini, choosing those packages where you can easily see that you are buying the mushroom not just the stem. Remember that they will need soaking for at least 30 minutes before use.

For the sauce
- 1oz dried porcini mushrooms
- 6 tbsp virgin olive oil
- 4 smoked or regular garlic cloves, peeled and thinly sliced
- 1 tbsp chopped fresh rosemary
- 1 tbsp chopped fresh sage
- 1½ cups trimmed and sliced mushrooms

- 4 tbsp dry white wine
- 8oz green beans, trimmed, sliced, and blanched

To serve
- 1lb fresh maltagliati
- freshly shaved Romano cheese
- sprigs of rosemary and sage

Soak the porcini in warm water for about 30 minutes. Drain, chop into small pieces, and reserve. Heat the oil in a pan and sauté the garlic for 2 minutes. Stir in the chopped herbs, porcini, and mushrooms and continue to sauté for 4 minutes. Add the wine and green beans, then bring to a boil. Reduce the heat, cover with a lid, and simmer for 3 minutes.

Meanwhile, cook the maltagliati in plenty of salted boiling water for 1-2 minutes or until "al dente." Drain and return to the pan. Add the sauce to the pasta and toss lightly. Serve immediately, topped with the freshly shaved cheese and sage and rosemary sprigs to garnish.

NUTRITION FACTS

Serving size 1 (266g)
Calories 629   Calories from fat 279

	% daily value *
Total fat 31g	47%
Saturated fat 6g	28%
Monounsaturated fat 19.4g	0%
Polyunsaturated fat 2.9g	0%
Cholesterol 153mg	51%
Sodium 288mg	12%
Total carbohydrate 70g	23%
Dietary fiber 5g	20%
Sugars 3g	0%
Protein 17g	0%

* Percent daily values are based on a 2,000-calorie diet

PASTA AND RATATOUILLE

Ratatouille is a classic Mediterranean dish; combine it with pasta and you have an all-time favorite. I have used canned tomatoes in this recipe but if you prefer you can use 1¹/₂ lb fresh peeled tomatoes and an extra tablespoon of tomato paste.

NUTRITION FACTS

Serving size 1 (395g)
Calories 484   Calories from fat 216

	% daily value *
Total fat 24g	36%
Saturated fat 6g	29%
Monounsaturated fat 13.9g	0%
Polyunsaturated fat 2.1g	0%
Cholesterol 111mg	37%
Sodium 595mg	25%
Total carbohydrate 51g	17%
Dietary fiber 5g	22%
Sugars 4g	0%
Protein 16g	0%

* Percent daily values are based on a 2,000-calorie diet

For the sauce

◆ 1 medium eggplant, trimmed and sliced
◆ salt
◆ 4 tbsp olive oil
◆ 1 large onion, peeled and thinly sliced
◆ 2-4 garlic cloves, peeled and chopped
◆ 1½ cups sliced zucchini
◆ 2 × 14oz cans chopped tomatoes
◆ 1 tbsp tomato paste

◆ 6 tbsp red wine
◆ ground black pepper
◆ 1 tbsp chopped fresh oregano
◆ 1 tbsp chopped fresh flat leaf parsley
◆ ¾ cup button mushrooms, wiped and halved

To serve

◆ 10oz fresh orecchiette
◆ ¾ cup sliced mozzarella cheese

Layer the eggplant in a colander, sprinkling between each layer with salt. Let sit 30 minutes. Drain, rinse well in cold water, and pat dry.

Heat the oil in a large pan and sauté the eggplant, onion, garlic, and zucchini for 5-8 minutes or until softened. (You may need to add a little more olive oil as the eggplant will tend to soak it up.)

Add the tomatoes. Blend the tomato paste with the wine and stir into the pan with the black pepper, oregano, parsley, and mushrooms.

Bring to a boil, reduce the heat, cover with a lid and simmer for 15 minutes or until the vegetables are tender but still retain a bite.

Meanwhile, cook the orecchiette in plenty of boiling salted water for 1-2 minutes or until "al dente." Drain and place in the base of an ovenproof gratin dish.

Pour over the prepared sauce and top with the sliced mozzarella cheese. Place under a medium hot broiler and cook for 5-8 minutes or until the cheese has melted and is golden.

Pasta and Ratatouille

Farfalle with Salmon

FARFALLE WITH SALMON

This is certainly one of my favorite recipes and is one that I inevitably fall back on when I have friends visit. It works equally well either as an appetizer or as a main meal if served with plenty of crusty bread and salad.

For the sauce
- 1½ cups broccoli flowerets
- 4 tbsp butter
- 2 cups thinly sliced leeks
- 4 plum tomatoes, peeled, seeded, and chopped
- ⅔ cup heavy whipping cream
- 8oz smoked salmon, cut into thin strips

To serve
- 1lb fresh farfalle
- ground black pepper

Divide the broccoli into tiny flowerets, then blanch in boiling water for 2 minutes. Drain and refresh in cold water. Reserve.

Melt the butter in a pan and sauté the leeks for 4 minutes, stirring frequently. Add the drained broccoli and tomatoes, cream, and smoked salmon and heat through, stirring occasionally. Cover with a lid and reserve.

Meanwhile, cook the farfalle in plenty of salted boiling water for 1-2 minutes or until "al dente." Drain and return to the pan. Add the cream and smoked salmon mixture. Toss lightly and serve immediately sprinkled with freshly ground black pepper.

NUTRITION FACTS

Serving size 1 (436g)
Calories 723   Calories from fat 333

	% daily value *
Total fat 37g	57%
Saturated fat 19g	94%
Monounsaturated fat 12.8g	0%
Polyunsaturated fat 2.94g	0%
Cholesterol 245mg	82%
Sodium 805mg	34%
Total carbohydrate 72g	24%
Dietary fiber 5g	22%
Sugars 9g	0%
Protein 26g	0%

* Percent daily values are based on a 2,000-calorie diet

GARGANELLI WITH EGGPLANTS

Eggplants come in many different shapes. There seems to be a growing trend to discard the idea of sprinkling the eggplant with salt prior to cooking and with the baby eggplant it certainly does not seem to be necessary.

For the sauce
- 6 tbsp olive oil
- 3 garlic cloves, peeled and thinly sliced
- 4 shallots, peeled and cut into thin wedges
- 4–5 baby eggplant, cut into small strips
- 1 small red bell pepper, seeded and chopped
- 1 small green bell pepper, seeded and chopped

- 2 x 14oz can chopped tomatoes
- 1 tbsp chopped fresh rosemary
- salt and ground black pepper

To serve
- 1lb fresh garganelli
- freshly grated Parmigiano Reggiano cheese

Heat the olive oil in a large pan and gently sauté the garlic, shallots, and eggplant strips for 10 minutes or until softened. Add the bell peppers and sauté for a further 2 minutes, then add the chopped tomatoes, rosemary, and seasoning to taste. Bring to a boil, reduce the heat, and simmer for 5-8 minutes or until a thick sauce consistency is reached.

Cook the garganelli in plenty of salted boiling water for 1-2 minutes or until "al dente." Drain and return to the pan. Add the eggplant and tomato sauce. Toss lightly and serve immediately with the grated cheese.

NUTRITION FACTS

Serving size 1 (411g)
Calories 605   Calories from fat 261

	% daily value *
Total fat 29g	45%
Saturated fat 5g	23%
Monounsaturated fat 18.9g	0%
Polyunsaturated fat 2.82g	0%
Cholesterol 147mg	49%
Sodium 575mg	24%
Total carbohydrate 72g	24%
Dietary fiber 6g	23%
Sugars 4g	0%
Protein 16g	0%

* Percent daily values are based on a 2,000-calorie diet

ORECCHIETTE WITH HERBS

You can vary the herbs that you use according to availability and personal taste. The flavor will be better if you finely chop the herbs rather than blending them to a paste in a food processor.

NUTRITION FACTS

Serving size 1 (158g)

Calories 557   Calories from fat 261

	% daily value *
Total fat 29g	45%
Saturated fat 11g	54%
Monounsaturated fat 11.9g	0%
Polyunsaturated fat 3.9g	0%
Cholesterol 179mg	60%
Sodium 340mg	14%
Total carbohydrate 60g	20%
Dietary fiber 3g	10%
Sugars 1g	0%
Protein 15g	0%

* Percent daily values are based on a 2,000-calorie diet

For the sauce

- 4 tbsp butter
- 2 garlic cloves, peeled and finely chopped
- 6 tbsp chopped fresh mixed herbs, such as basil, oregano, flat leaf parsley, chives, rosemary, and sage
- grated rind and juice of 1 lemon
- ¼ cup toasted pine nuts
- 1 tbsp extra virgin olive oil

Melt the butter in a pan and sauté the garlic for 3 minutes. Add the herbs and lemon rind and juice, and continue to sauté for 2 minutes. Stir in the toasted pine nuts.

Meanwhile, cook the orecchiette in plenty of salted boiling water for 1-2 minutes or until "al dente." Drain, reserving 2 tablespoons of the cooking liquor.

To serve

- 1lb fresh orecchiette
- freshly shaved Parmigiano Reggiano to serve

Return the pasta to the pan with the cooking liquor and add the herb sauce and olive oil. Toss lightly and serve immediately with the freshly shaved Parmigiano Reggiano cheese.

BRANDELLE GENOESE

This sauce will work as well with any of the prepared homemade unfilled pastas as with ravioli or tortelloni.

NUTRITION FACTS

Serving size 1 (342g)

Calories 620   Calories from fat 234

	% daily value *
Total fat 26g	41%
Saturated fat 6g	30%
Monounsaturated fat 15.6g	0%
Polyunsaturated fat 2.6g	0%
Cholesterol 246mg	82%
Sodium 583mg	24%
Total carbohydrate 75g	25%
Dietary fiber 6g	23%
Sugars 12g	0%
Protein 22g	0%

* Percent daily values are based on a 2,000-calorie diet

For the sauce

- 4 tbsp olive oil
- 1 large onion, peeled and chopped
- 2 garlic cloves, peeled and finely chopped
- 2½ cups puréed tomatoes
- 1 tbsp roughly torn fresh basil
- salt and ground black pepper
- 2 medium eggs, beaten

Heat the oil in a large pan and sauté the onion and garlic for 8 minutes or until very soft. Pour in the puréed tomatoes and bring to a boil. Reduce the heat and simmer for 10 minutes. Add the basil leaves and seasoning to taste.

Meanwhile, cook the brandelle in plenty of salted boiling water for 1-2 minutes or until "al dente." Drain.

To serve

- 1lb fresh brandelle
- ½ cup freshly grated Parmesan cheese

Gently reheat the sauce and, without allowing the sauce to boil, whisk in the eggs. Cook gently, whisking throughout until the sauce thickens. Add the pasta and Parmesan cheese, toss lightly, and serve immediately.

Orecchiette with Herbs

MALTAGLIATI WITH LAMB AND CHIVES

If preferred you can use ground lamb, but I prefer to buy leg of lamb and chop the meat very finely.

For the sauce
- 3 tbsp olive oil
- 2 garlic cloves, peeled and finely chopped
- 1 large onion, peeled and chopped
- 10oz lean lamb, trimmed and finely chopped
- 14oz can chopped tomatoes
- 1 tbsp tomato paste
- 4 tbsp red wine
- 1 tbsp snipped fresh chives
- salt and ground black pepper

To serve
- 1lb fresh maltagliati
- 2-3 tbsp freshly grated Parmesan cheese
- extra snipped fresh chives

Heat the oil in a pan and sauté the garlic and onion for 5 minutes or until softened. Add the lamb and continue to sauté for 5 minutes, stirring frequently, until browned.

Add the chopped tomatoes, the tomato paste blended with 2 tablespoons water, and the red wine. Bring to a boil, reduce the heat, cover with a lid, and simmer for 40 minutes or until a thick sauce is formed. Add the snipped chives and seasoning to taste, and continue to simmer for 5 minutes while cooking the pasta.

Cook the pasta in plenty of salted boiling water for 1-2 minutes or until "al dente." Drain and return to the pan. Add the meat sauce, toss lightly, then serve sprinkled with the grated Parmesan cheese and extra snipped fresh chives.

MALTAGLIATI WITH ASPARAGUS AND BABY CORN

Maltagliati means torn or badly cut, so its shape works well with asparagus and baby corn after they have been cut into shorter lengths. For vegetarians, just leave out the Parma ham and add a few extra toasted pine nuts.

For the sauce
- 4 tbsp butter
- 1 white onion, peeled and thinly sliced
- 8–10 asparagus spears, trimmed, woody part discarded and cut into 2-inch lengths
- 1 cup canned baby corn, cut into 2-inch lengths
- 1 scant cup heavy whipping cream
- ¼ cup toasted pine nuts
- 1 tbsp chopped fresh basil
- 3oz Parma ham, shredded
- salt and ground black pepper
- ¼ cup freshly grated Parmesan cheese

To serve
- 1lb fresh maltagliati

Melt the butter in a pan and gently sauté the onion for 5 minutes or until softened. Add the asparagus spears and continue to sauté for 2 minutes, then add the corn and cream.

Bring the cream mixture to a boil, reduce the heat, and simmer for 2 minutes. Stir in the pine nuts, basil, Parma ham, seasoning to taste, and cheese. Heat through, stirring, then cover with a lid and remove from the heat.

Meanwhile, cook the fresh maltagliati in plenty of salted boiling water for 1-2 minutes or until "al dente." Drain and return to the pan. Add the sauce to the pasta, toss lightly, then serve immediately.

Maltagliati with Lamb and Chives

Macaroni with Bell and Chile Peppers and Opal Basil

MACARONI WITH BELL AND CHILE PEPPERS AND OPAL BASIL

When using chile peppers take care as their heat level can be deceptive. Remove the seeds as well as the membrane that the seeds are attached to. As a general guide, remember, the smaller the chile the hotter the heat level.

For the sauce
- 2 red bell peppers, seeded
- 2 yellow bell peppers, seeded
- 2 green bell peppers, seeded
- 1-3 jalapeño chiles, seeded
- 4 tbsp olive oil
- 1 large onion, peeled and finely sliced
- 3 smoked or regular garlic cloves, peeled and finely sliced
- 2 cups puréed tomatoes
- salt and ground black pepper
- few sprigs of opal basil

To serve
- 1lb fresh macaroni
- sprigs of opal basil
- freshly grated Romano cheese

Heat the broiler to high then charbroil the bell peppers and chile peppers for 10 minutes or until the skins have blistered. Remove from the heat and place in a plastic bag until cool. Peel and cut into thin strips.

Heat the oil in a large pan and sauté the onion and garlic for 5 minutes or until softened. Add the peppers with the puréed tomatoes and bring to a boil. Cover with a lid, reduce the heat, and simmer for 5-8 minutes or until the sauce has thickened. Add the seasoning to taste and the basil sprigs.

Meanwhile, cook the macaroni in plenty of salted boiling water for 1-2 minutes or until "al dente." Drain and return to the pan. Add the prepared sauce and toss lightly. Serve immediately garnished with the opal basil sprigs and handing the grated cheese separately.

NUTRITION FACTS

Serving size 1 (540g)
Calories 594   Calories from fat 207

	% daily value *
Total fat 23g	36%
Saturated fat 5g	24%
Monounsaturated fat 14.4g	0%
Polyunsaturated fat 2.3g	0%
Cholesterol 153mg	51%
Sodium 485mg	20%
Total carbohydrate 80g	27%
Dietary fiber 9g	37%
Sugars 17g	0%
Protein 19g	0%

* Percent daily values are based on a 2,000-calorie diet

FARFALLE WITH MORTADELLA

One tip that I learnt early on when cooking pasta is to save some of the pasta cooking liquor. It is the best way to moisten the pasta or to thin the sauce if it has become too thick. So when draining the cooked pasta, always keep a little until you have served the dish.

For the sauce
- 3 tbsp olive oil
- 2 cups sliced leeks
- 2-3 garlic cloves, peeled and cut into thin slivers
- 14oz can chopped tomatoes
- ⅔ cup red wine
- 6oz mortadella, sliced and cut into thin strips
- 2 tbsp chopped fresh flat leaf parsley

To serve
- 1lb fresh farfalle
- freshly grated Romano cheese

Heat the oil in a pan and sauté the leeks and garlic for 5 minutes. Add the contents of the can of tomatoes and the red wine.

Bring to a boil, reduce the heat, and cover with a lid. Simmer for 10 minutes or until the sauce has been reduced by about half or until a thick consistency is reached. Add the strips of mortadella to the sauce and simmer gently while cooking the pasta.

Cook the farfalle in plenty of boiling salted water for 1-2 minutes or until "al dente." Drain and return to the pan. Add the sauce and parsley, then toss lightly. Serve immediately, handing the grated cheese separately.

NUTRITION FACTS

Serving size 1 (368g)
Calories 678   Calories from fat 279

	% daily value *
Total fat 31g	47%
Saturated fat 8g	42%
Monounsaturated fat 16.7g	0%
Polyunsaturated fat 3.38g	0%
Cholesterol 177mg	59%
Sodium 1027mg	43%
Total carbohydrate 70g	23%
Dietary fiber 4g	16%
Sugars 4g	0%
Protein 24g	0%

* Percent daily values are based on a 2,000-calorie diet

MALTAGLIATI WITH ANCHOVIES

When using anchovies, soak in a little milk for about 30 minutes before using, then drain and pat dry. This removes any excess salt and helps provide the healthier diet that is so desirable today. The combination of red onion, cabbage, and snow peas makes for a very colorful dish.

NUTRITION FACTS

Serving size 1 (328g)
Calories 583   Calories from fat 198

	% daily value *
Total fat 22g	34%
Saturated fat 5g	25%
Monounsaturated fat 12.8g	0%
Polyunsaturated fat 2.45g	0%
Cholesterol 177mg	59%
Sodium 879mg	37%
Total carbohydrate 69g	23%
Dietary fiber 6g	22%
Sugars 8g	0%
Protein 27g	0%

* Percent daily values are based on a 2,000-calorie diet

For the sauce
◆ 1½ cups snow peas
◆ 3 tbsp olive oil
◆ 1 red onion, peeled and finely sliced
◆ 2 garlic cloves, peeled and finely chopped
◆ 4oz sliced Parma ham, cut into thin strips
◆ 1½ cups finely shredded green cabbage

◆ 2oz can anchovy fillets, drained and soaked in milk for 30 minutes
◆ salt and ground black pepper

To serve
◆ 1lb fresh maltagliati
◆ freshly shaved Romano cheese

Cook the peas in lightly salted boiling water for 2-3 minutes or until tender, drain and reserve. Heat the oil in a pan and sauté the onion and garlic for 5 minutes or until softened. Add the peas, ham, and cabbage and continue to sauté for a further 3 minutes.

Meanwhile, cook the pasta in plenty of salted boiling water for 1-2 minutes or until "al dente." Drain, reserving 4 tablespoons of the liquor.

Add the pasta liquor to the onion, pea, and ham mixture together with the anchovy fillets and seasoning to taste. Add the cooked pasta to the mixture. Toss lightly before serving with the freshly shaved cheese.

ORECCHIETTE WITH SAUSAGE AND PANCETTA

Pancetta is cured in the same way as prosciutto but is not matured for as long and is generally unsmoked. If you can not find pancetta, use smoked bacon.

NUTRITION FACTS

Serving size 1 (507g)
Calories 945   Calories from fat 486

	% daily value *
Total fat 54g	83%
Saturated fat 22g	108%
Monounsaturated fat 14.3g	0%
Polyunsaturated fat 3.44g	0%
Cholesterol 257mg	86%
Sodium 1345mg	56%
Total carbohydrate 70g	24%
Dietary fiber 5g	18%
Sugars 8g	0%
Protein 34g	0%

* Percent daily values are based on a 2,000-calorie diet

For the sauce
◆ 4 tbsp butter
◆ 1 onion, peeled and sliced
◆ 4oz pancetta, thinly chopped
◆ 1 cup pork sausage
◆ 1¼ cups red wine
◆ few sprigs sage

◆ 8 plum tomatoes, peeled, seeded, and chopped
◆ ¼ tsp freshly grated nutmeg

To serve
◆ 1lb fresh orecchiette
◆ freshly grated Parmigiano Reggiano cheese

Melt the butter in a pan and sauté the onion and pancetta for 5 minutes or until the onion has softened and the pancetta has become golden. Roll the sausage into small balls. Add to the pan and sauté for 5 minutes or until browned. Add the wine, sage, and tomatoes. Bring to a boil, cover with a lid, and simmer for 5 minutes, stirring occasionally.

Meanwhile, cook the orecchiette in plenty of salted boiling water for 1-2 minutes or until "al dente." Drain and return to the pan. Add the nutmeg to the sauce and pour over the pasta. Toss lightly and serve immediately sprinkled with the cheese.

Maltagliati with Anchovies

Beef Stew with Pasta

BEEF STEW WITH PASTA

This recipe is based on the Corsican Stufatu, *but I have added a few extra ingredients to make it a hearty and filling dish.*

For the sauce
◆ 2 tbsp olive oil
◆ 1 large onion, peeled and chopped
◆ 2-3 garlic cloves, peeled and minced
◆ 1lb chuck steak, trimmed and diced
◆ 2 tbsp seasoned flour
◆ ⅔ cup red wine
◆ 2 cups beef stock
◆ salt and ground black pepper

◆ 2 tbsp chopped fresh oregano
◆ 4–6 baby carrots, trimmed
◆ 2 cups leeks, blanched and sliced

To serve
◆ 10oz fresh fusilli
◆ freshly grated Parmesan cheese
◆ chopped fresh oregano

Preheat the oven to 350°F, 10 minutes before cooking the stew. Heat the oil in a large pan and sauté the onion and garlic for 5 minutes or until softened but not browned.

Toss the meat in the seasoned flour, then add to the pan and brown, stirring frequently. Sprinkle in any remaining flour and cook for 2 minutes. Gradually stir in the wine and stock. Bring to a boil, stirring, then remove from the heat and stir in seasoning to taste and the oregano. Pour into a casserole dish, cover with a lid, and cook for 1½ hours.

Cut the carrots in half if large. Cook in boiling water for 3 minutes, drain, and add to the stew with the leeks. Continue to cook for 30 minutes or until the meat is tender.

Meanwhile, cook the fusilli in plenty of salted boiling water for 1-2 minutes or until "al dente." Drain and stir into the stew. Sprinkle with the grated Parmesan and oregano and serve.

NUTRITION FACTS

Serving size 1 (623g)
Calories 959   Calories from fat 297

	% daily value *
Total fat 33g	51%
Saturated fat 10g	52%
Monounsaturated fat 16.4g	0%
Polyunsaturated fat 2.85g	0%
Cholesterol 162mg	54%
Sodium 822mg	34%
Total carbohydrate 118g	39%
Dietary fiber 7g	29%
Sugars 12g	0%
Protein 39g	0%

* Percent daily values are based on a 2,000-calorie diet

BRANDELLE WITH PORCINI AND ANCHOVIES

As this is based on the famous pesto sauce, treat it in exactly the same way. Store in the refrigerator in a screw top jar. Dispel any air bubbles and cover with a thin layer of olive oil. Consume within 24 hours.

For the sauce
◆ ½oz dried porcini
◆ 6-8 tbsp olive oil
◆ 2 firm tomatoes, peeled, seeded, and chopped
◆ ½ cup pine nuts
◆ 4 garlic cloves
◆ small bunch basil leaves

◆ 4 anchovy fillets, soaked in milk for 30 minutes, chopped

To serve
◆ 1lb fresh brandelle
◆ freshly shaved Parmigiano Reggiano

Soak the porcini in warm water for about 30 minutes. Drain, reserving the soaking liquor, and chop the porcini. Heat 2 tablespoons of the oil in a pan and gently sauté the porcini for 2 minutes. Strain the soaking liquid, then add to the porcini and cook until the liquid has almost evaporated. Add the tomatoes and heat for 1 minute.

Place the mushroom mixture with the pine nuts, garlic, basil leaves, and anchovies in a food processor. Blend for 1 minute. With the motor still running, gradually pour in the remaining oil until a thick paste is formed.

Meanwhile, cook the brandelle in plenty of salted boiling water for 1-2 minutes or until "al dente." Drain and return to the pan. Add the mushroom paste and toss lightly until the pasta is coated. Serve immediately sprinkled with the shaved Parmigiano Reggiano.

NUTRITION FACTS

Serving size 1 (227g)
Calories 697   Calories from fat 378

	% daily value *
Total fat 42g	65%
Saturated fat 7g	34%
Monounsaturated fat 25.4g	0%
Polyunsaturated fat 7.5g	0%
Cholesterol 150mg	50%
Sodium 368mg	15%
Total carbohydrate 65g	22%
Dietary fiber 4g	16%
Sugars 3g	0%
Protein 19g	0%

* Percent daily values are based on a 2,000-calorie diet

PASTA LAMB BAKE

This dish can be made ahead of time and cooked later. If doing this, I would recommend that you make the sauce slightly thinner as, while it sits, the pasta will soak up more of the sauce than if you cook it immediately.

NUTRITION FACTS

Serving size 1 (328g)
Calories 571   Calories from fat 225

	% daily value *
Total fat 25g	38%
Saturated fat 8g	42%
Monounsaturated fat 12.3g	0%
Polyunsaturated fat 1.99g	0%
Cholesterol 145mg	48%
Sodium 404mg	17%
Total carbohydrate 54g	18%
Dietary fiber 5g	19%
Sugars 7g	0%
Protein 29g	0%

* Percent daily values are based on a 2,000-calorie diet

For the sauce
◆ 8oz lean lamb
◆ 2 tbsp olive oil
◆ 1 onion, peeled and chopped
◆ 2 garlic cloves, peeled and minced
◆ 8 sun-dried tomatoes, chopped
◆ 1 red bell pepper, seeded and chopped
◆ ⅔ cup red wine

◆ 1¼ cups puréed tomatoes
◆ 1 tbsp chopped fresh oregano
◆ salt and ground black pepper

To serve
◆ 8oz fresh farfalle
◆ ¾ cup grated mozzarella cheese

Preheat the oven to 375°F, 10 minutes before baking the pasta dish. Trim the lamb and dice.

Heat the oil in a skillet and sauté the onion, garlic, sun-dried tomatoes, and red pepper for 5 minutes or until softened. Add the lamb and sauté for a further 3 minutes or until sealed. Add the red wine, puréed tomatoes, and oregano with seasoning to taste. Simmer for 5 minutes, then remove from the heat.

Meanwhile, cook the farfalle in plenty of salted boiling water for 1 minute or until almost "al dente." Drain and return to the pan. Add the lamb and sauce and toss lightly.

Spoon the mixture into an ovenproof dish and top with the grated mozzarella cheese. Bake the pasta dish in the preheated oven for 20 minutes or until the cheese has melted and is golden and bubbly.

FARFALLE WITH TURKEY AND PORCINI

Turkey is traditionally reserved for special occasions, which seems a great shame. As turkey is so low in fat, we really should be eating more of it.

NUTRITION FACTS

Serving size 1 (314g)
Calories 571   Calories from fat 171

	% daily value *
Total fat 19g	29%
Saturated fat 3g	17%
Monounsaturated fat 11.6g	0%
Polyunsaturated fat 2.1g	0%
Cholesterol 194mg	65%
Sodium 393mg	16%
Total carbohydrate 65g	22%
Dietary fiber 4g	18%
Sugars 4g	0%
Protein 31g	0%

* Percent daily values are based on a 2,000-calorie diet

For the sauce
◆ 1oz dried porcini
◆ 1 red bell pepper, seeded
◆ 1 green bell pepper, seeded
◆ 3 tbsp olive oil
◆ 2 garlic cloves, peeled and thinly sliced
◆ 8oz turkey breast meat, trimmed and thinly sliced
◆ 1 cup button mushrooms, wiped and sliced

◆ 6 tbsp dry white wine
◆ salt and ground black pepper
◆ 2 tbsp chopped fresh flat leaf parsley

To serve
◆ 1lb fresh farfalle
◆ freshly shaved Parmigiano Reggiano

Soak the porcini in warm water for about 30 minutes. Drain, chop finely, and reserve.

Preheat the broiler to high, then charbroil the peppers for 10 minutes or until the skins have blistered. Remove from the heat; place in a plastic bag until cool. Skin and cut into thin strips.

Heat the oil in a pan and sauté the garlic and turkey for 5 minutes or until the turkey is sealed. Add the chopped porcini and button mushrooms and continue to sauté for 3 more minutes.

Add the pepper strips and wine to the pan and simmer for 5 minutes. Stir in the seasoning to taste and chopped parsley. Cover with a lid and remove from the heat while cooking the fresh farfalle.

Cook the farfalle in plenty of salted boiling water for 1-2 minutes or until "al dente." Drain and place on a warm serving plate. Top with the reserved turkey mixture and serve sprinkled with the shaved cheese.

Pasta Lamb Bake

FUSILLI WITH ARTICHOKES

When in season fresh globe artichokes are superb, but unfortunately they are one of the few vegetables that are not available all year round. This recipe overcomes the problem by using canned artichoke hearts.

For the sauce
◆ 3 tbsp olive oil
◆ 1 red onion, peeled and cut into thin wedges
◆ 4oz Parma ham, cut about ¼ inch thick
◆ 14oz can artichoke hearts, drained
◆ 1 cup halved cherry tomatoes

◆ juice of 1 lemon
◆ 6 tbsp heavy whipping cream

To serve
◆ 1lb fresh fusilli
◆ freshly grated Romano cheese

Heat the oil in a pan and sauté the onion for 5 minutes or until softened. Discard any excess fat from the ham and cut into strips. Drain the artichokes and cut into quarters. Add to the pan with the ham, tomatoes, and lemon juice.

Bring to a boil, cover with a lid, and simmer for 5 minutes or until heated through. Stir in the cream. Heat through, then cover with the lid and remove from the heat.

Meanwhile, cook the fusilli in plenty of salted boiling water for 1-2 minutes or until "al dente." Drain and return to the pan. Add the artichoke mixture and toss lightly. Serve, handing the grated cheese separately.

ORECCHIETTE WITH FOUR CHEESES

Vary the cheese used according to personal taste, but make sure you use at least one of the stringy varieties such as Gruyère or Emmenthal.

For the sauce
◆ 2oz Gruyère cheese
◆ 2oz Gorgonzola or Dolcelatte cheese
◆ 2oz smoked mozzarella cheese
◆ ½ cup freshly grated Romano cheese
◆ 4 tbsp butter
◆ 2 celery stems, trimmed and finely chopped

◆ 8 scallions, trimmed and diagonally sliced
◆ ½ cup walnut halves, roughly chopped

To serve
◆ 1lb fresh orecchiette
◆ sprigs of flat leaf parsley
◆ grated lemon rind

Cut the Gruyère, Gorgonzola or Dolcelatte, and mozzarella cheese into very small cubes. Place in a bowl with the Romano cheese, mix, and reserve.

Melt the butter in a pan and gently sauté the celery for 3 minutes. Add the scallions and sauté for 1-2 minutes or until softened. Add the walnuts, mix, cover with a lid, and remove from the heat.

Meanwhile, cook the orecchiette in plenty of salted boiling water for 1-2 minutes or until "al dente." Drain and return to the pan. Add the reserved cheeses and the scallion mixture. Toss lightly and heat gently until the cheese begins to melt. Serve immediately garnished with the flat leaf parsley and grated lemon rind.

CHAPTER FIVE

LONG AND RIBBON PASTA

The long pasta varieties are perhaps the easiest to make. The sauce should just coat the pasta, so that you retain the balance of tastes and textures. There are many different types with varying widths and lengths. In Italy their names can vary from region to region but collectively they are all known as "pasta lunga."

TAGLIATELLE WITH GARLIC AND MIXED SEAFOOD

There is a great abundance of seafood along the coastline of Italy, and the combination of fish and pasta is truly magnificent.

NUTRITION FACTS

Serving size 1 (350g)
Calories 536   Calories from fat 225

	% daily value *
Total fat 25g	38%
Saturated fat 3g	17%
Monounsaturated fat 15.4g	0%
Polyunsaturated fat 3.1g	0%
Cholesterol 319mg	106%
Sodium 500mg	21%
Total carbohydrate 34g	11%
Dietary fiber 1g	3%
Sugars 2g	0%
Protein 39g	0%

* Percent daily values are based on a 2,000-calorie diet

For the sauce
- 12 fresh clams in their shells
- 16 fresh mussels in their shells
- 8oz large raw shrimp
- 8oz squid
- 6 tbsp virgin olive oil
- 2-3 garlic cloves, peeled and minced
- 1-2 serrano chiles, seeded and chopped
- ½ cup dry white wine
- salt and ground black pepper

To serve
- 1lb fresh tagliatelle
- flat leaf parsley
- freshly chopped chile

Scrub the clams and mussels, discarding any barnacles and beards from the shells. Soak in cold water for 30 minutes. Discard any that are open. Shell and devein the shrimp. Clean the squid and cut into rings.

Heat the oil in a large pan and gently sauté the garlic and chiles for 5 minutes or until softened but not browned. Add the prepared seafood and cook for 5-8 minutes, stirring. Pour in the wine and cook for 2-3 minutes. Discard any clams or mussels that have not opened.

Meanwhile, cook the tagliatelle in plenty of boiling salted water for 1-2 minutes or until "al dente." Drain. Season the sauce and add to the pasta. Toss lightly, garnish with the parsley and chile, and serve immediately.

TURKEY BOLOGNESE

When most people think of spaghetti they automatically think of Spaghetti Bolognese, which of course uses the traditional Ragu sauce. However, this sauce can easily be adapted by using other types of ground meat. Turkey is one of the healthiest of meats and makes a delicious sauce to serve with spaghetti.

NUTRITION FACTS

Serving size 1 (461g)
Calories 613   Calories from fat 198

	% daily value *
Total fat 22g	33%
Saturated fat 5g	23%
Monounsaturated fat 11.3g	0%
Polyunsaturated fat 3.1g	0%
Cholesterol 204mg	68%
Sodium 715mg	30%
Total carbohydrate 69g	23%
Dietary fiber 6g	25%
Sugars 6g	0%
Protein 28g	0%

* Percent daily values are based on a 2,000-calorie diet

For the sauce
- 2 tbsp olive oil
- 1 onion, peeled and chopped
- 2-3 garlic cloves, peeled and finely chopped
- 1 serrano chile, seeded and chopped
- 1 small red bell pepper, seeded and finely chopped
- 2 celery stems, trimmed and finely chopped
- 1½ cups finely diced carrots
- 10oz fresh ground turkey
- 14oz can chopped tomatoes
- 2 tbsp tomato paste
- ⅔ cup dry white wine
- salt and ground black pepper
- 1 tbsp chopped fresh oregano

To serve
- 1lb fresh spaghetti
- 1 tbsp chopped fresh oregano
- freshly grated Parmesan cheese

Heat the oil in a skillet and sauté the onion, garlic, chile, red bell pepper, celery, and carrots for 5-6 minutes or until the onion is softened. Add the turkey and continue to sauté for 5 minutes, stirring, or until the turkey is sealed.

Add the contents of the can of tomatoes. Blend the tomato paste with the wine and stir into the pan. Season to taste and add 1 tablespoon of chopped oregano. Bring to a boil, reduce the heat, cover with a lid, and simmer for 15 minutes or until the sauce has thickened.

Meanwhile, cook the spaghetti in plenty of salted boiling water for 1-2 minutes or until "al dente." Drain and return to the pan. Add the sauce and toss lightly. Serve sprinkled with the oregano. Hand the grated cheese separately.

Tagliatelle with Garlic and Mixed Seafood

SPAGHETTI WITH SHRIMP AND ASPARAGUS

When serving pasta, it is important to remember that it should never be served swimming in sauce—the sauce should just coat the strands of pasta. If you prefer, you can blanch the asparagus for this dish, but personally I prefer a slightly crunchy texture.

For the sauce
◆ 8–10 fresh asparagus spears, trimmed
◆ 2 tbsp butter
◆ 2 shallots, peeled and chopped
◆ 1-2 garlic cloves, peeled and cut into thin slivers
◆ 8oz raw shrimp, shelled and deveined

◆ scant 1 cup heavy whipping cream
◆ salt and ground black pepper

To serve
◆ 1lb fresh spaghetti

Cut the asparagus into 1 inch pieces. Melt the butter in a pan and sauté the shallots and garlic for 5 minutes or until softened. Add the asparagus and sauté for 2 minutes.

Add the shrimp and cook, stirring, over a medium heat until the shrimp have turned pink. Stir in the cream. Continue to cook until the cream has reduced by about half. Cover with a lid and remove from the heat.

Meanwhile, cook the spaghetti in plenty of salted boiling water for 1-2 minutes or until "al dente." Drain and return the pasta to the pan. Pour in the sauce and toss lightly. Season to taste and serve immediately.

FETTUCCINE WITH FENNEL AND ROASTED PEPPER SAUCE

When using fennel, always keep the feathery fronds as they make an excellent garnish for the finished dish. The combination of smoked garlic with the aniseed flavor of the fennel is delicous.

For the sauce
◆ 2 red bell peppers, seeded and cut into four
◆ 2 yellow bell peppers, seeded and cut into four
◆ 6 tbsp olive oil
◆ salt and ground black pepper
◆ 1 large fennel bulb, trimmed
◆ 4-5 smoked or regular garlic cloves, peeled and cut into thin slivers

To serve
◆ 1lb fresh fettuccine
◆ few sprigs of basil
◆ fennel fronds
◆ 4 tbsp freshly grated Parmigiano Reggiano cheese

Preheat the broiler and charbroil the red and yellow peppers for 10 minutes or until the skins have blistered. Remove from the heat and place in a plastic bag. Let sit 10 minutes, then peel and discard the skins.

Place the peppers with 3 tablespoons of the oil in a food processor and blend to form a smooth purée. Season to taste and reserve.

Slice the fennel into thin strips. Heat the remaining oil in a skillet and gently sauté the fennel and garlic for 5-8 minutes or until the fennel is soft, stirring occasionally. Add the prepared pepper sauce and heat through gently.

Meanwhile, cook the fettuccine in plenty of boiling salted water for 1-2 minutes or until "al dente." Drain well and return the pasta to the pan. Pour in the sauce and toss lightly. Serve immediately garnished with basil sprigs and fennel fronds. Serve the grated cheese separately.

Spaghetti with Shrimp and Asparagus

Tagliatelle with Vegetables in Fresh Tomato Sauce

TAGLIATELLE WITH VEGETABLES IN FRESH TOMATO SAUCE

The Mediterranean has an abundance of vegetables. Choose any combination you wish, but use those whose colors and flavors are compatible with each other.

For the sauce
- 1 red bell pepper, seeded
- 1 yellow bell pepper, seeded
- 2 tbsp butter
- 1 large onion, peeled and cut into thin wedges
- 2-3 garlic cloves, peeled and minced
- 1½ cups diced zucchini
- 1lb plum tomatoes, peeled, seeded, and chopped
- 8 tbsp dry white wine
- 2 tbsp tomato paste
- 2 tbsp chopped fresh basil
- salt and ground black pepper

To serve
- 1lb fresh tagliatelle
- freshly shaved Parmigiano Reggiano cheese

Preheat the broiler to high and charbroil the peppers for 10 minutes. Remove from the broiler and place in a plastic bag. Let sit 10 minutes, then peel and cut into strips.

Melt the butter in a large pan and sauté the onion and garlic for 5 minutes. Add the zucchini and sauté for 2 minutes. Stir in the chopped tomatoes, wine, and tomato paste. Bring to a boil, reduce the heat, and cook for 5-8 minutes. Stir in the sliced peppers with the basil and seasoning to taste. Continue to simmer gently while cooking the pasta.

Cook the tagliatelle in plenty of salted boiling water for 1-2 minutes or until "al dente." Drain and add the pasta to the sauce, toss lightly, and serve with the shaved cheese.

NUTRITION FACTS

Serving size 1 (432g)
Calories 293   Calories from fat 72

	% daily value *
Total fat 8g	13%
Saturated fat 4g	21%
Monounsaturated fat 2.1g	0%
Polyunsaturated fat 0.9g	0%
Cholesterol 55mg	18%
Sodium 276mg	12%
Total carbohydrate 43g	14%
Dietary fiber 4g	16%
Sugars 10g	0%
Protein 9g	0%

* Percent daily values are based on a 2,000-calorie diet

TAGLIATELLE WITH PROSCIUTTO AND TOMATOES

Prosciutto is an air and salt-cured ham that imparts an unique and special flavor. If it is unavailable use smoked bacon, but the flavor will be slightly different.

For the sauce
- 4 tbsp butter
- 4oz prosciutto, thinly sliced and cut into strips
- 4 ripe plum tomatoes, seeded, peeled if preferred, and chopped
- 1 cup snow peas, trimmed and halved
- scant 1 cup heavy whipping cream
- ¼ cup freshly grated Parmigiano Reggiano cheese
- salt and ground black pepper

To serve
- 1lb fresh tagliatelle

Melt the butter in a large pan and sauté the prosciutto for 5 minutes, stirring occasionally. Add the tomatoes with the snow peas and cook for 2 minutes.

Add the cream and cook for 3 minutes, stirring. Stir in half the cheese with seasoning to taste. Cover with a lid, remove from the heat, and keep warm.

Meanwhile, cook the tagliatelle in plenty of salted boiling water for 1-2 minutes or until "al dente." Drain and return to the pan. Pour in the sauce and toss lightly. Serve sprinkled with the remaining grated cheese.

NUTRITION FACTS

Serving size 1 (378g)
Calories 609   Calories from fat 396

	% daily value *
Total fat 44g	67%
Saturated fat 25g	124%
Monounsaturated fat 13.3g	0%
Polyunsaturated fat 2.6g	0%
Cholesterol 174mg	58%
Sodium 914mg	38%
Total carbohydrate 39g	13%
Dietary fiber 2g	9%
Sugars 7g	0%
Protein 18g	0%

* Percent daily values are based on a 2,000-calorie diet

Angel Hair with Tuna and Olives

ANGEL HAIR WITH TUNA AND OLIVES

When black olives are used in a recipe you will often find capers, too. For a far superior flavor, look for capers that have been preserved in salt rather than vinegar or brine, then soak them in cold water for at least 30 minutes before use.

For the sauce
- 4 tbsp olive oil
- 2 leeks, trimmed and thinly sliced
- 1-2 smoked or regular garlic cloves, peeled and finely chopped
- 14oz can chopped tomatoes
- 1-2 tbsp tomato paste
- 2 × 7oz cans tuna, drained
- ½ cup pitted and halved black olives
- 2 tbsp capers
- salt and ground black pepper

To serve
- 1lb fresh angel hair pasta
- fresh sprigs of basil

Heat the oil in a pan and sauté the leeks and garlic for 5 minutes or until softened but not browned. Add the contents of the can of tomatoes and the tomato paste blended with ²/₃ cup water. Bring to a boil, cover with a lid, and simmer for 10 minutes or until a thick sauce consistency is reached. Add the tuna, olives, capers, and seasoning to taste. Heat through gently for 5 minutes.

Meanwhile, cook the angel hair pasta in plenty of salted boiling water for 1-2 minutes or until "al dente." Drain well and return to the pan. Add the sauce to the pasta and toss lightly. Serve immediately, garnished with the basil sprigs.

NUTRITION FACTS

Serving size 1 (417g)
Calories 658   Calories from fat 189

	% daily value *
Total fat 21g	32%
Saturated fat 4g	18%
Monounsaturated fat 10.1g	0%
Polyunsaturated fat 1.57g	0%
Cholesterol 157mg	52%
Sodium 1057mg	44%
Total carbohydrate 75g	25%
Dietary fiber 5g	21%
Sugars 5g	0%
Protein 42g	0%

* Percent daily values are based on a 2,000-calorie diet

FETTUCCINE WITH MEAT SAUCE

There are many different variations to the classic Bolognese meat sauce; all are equally delicious. I especially like this recipe as the pancetta adds to the flavor.

For the sauce
- 4 tbsp olive oil
- 1 onion, peeled and finely chopped
- 1 celery stem, trimmed and finely chopped
- 1 carrot, peeled and finely diced
- 2oz pancetta, thinly sliced and diced
- 10oz lean ground beef
- ²/₃ cup red wine
- ²/₃ cup beef stock
- salt and ground black pepper
- 1 tbsp chopped fresh marjoram

To serve
- 1lb fresh fettuccine
- freshly shaved Romano cheese

Heat the oil in a pan and sauté the onion, celery, carrot, and pancetta for 5-8 minutes or until softened but not browned. Add the beef and continue to sauté, stirring frequently to break up any lumps, for 5 minutes or until sealed.

Add the wine, stock, seasoning, and marjoram. Bring to a boil, reduce the heat, and simmer, stirring occasionally, for 12-15 minutes or until the sauce has thickened.

Meanwhile, cook the fettuccine in plenty of salted boiling water for 1-2 minutes or until "al dente." Drain and return to the pan. Add the sauce, toss lightly, and serve immediately, handing the shaved cheese separately.

NUTRITION FACTS

Serving size 1 (326g)
Calories 812   Calories from fat 405

	% daily value *
Total fat 45g	69%
Saturated fat 13g	66%
Monounsaturated fat 24.2g	0%
Polyunsaturated fat 3.82g	0%
Cholesterol 219mg	73%
Sodium 850mg	35%
Total carbohydrate 61g	20%
Dietary fiber 3g	12%
Sugars 3g	0%
Protein 32g	0%

* Percent daily values are based on a 2,000-calorie diet

ANGEL HAIR PASTA WITH SCALLOPS

Because angel hair pasta and scallops need so little cooking, this dish is quickly prepared; it is ready in about 5 minutes.

NUTRITION FACTS

Serving size 1 (347g)
Calories 751   Calories from fat 342

	% daily value *
Total fat 38g	59%
Saturated fat 22g	110%
Monounsaturated fat 9.6g	0%
Polyunsaturated fat 1.48g	0%
Cholesterol 266mg	89%
Sodium 577mg	24%
Total carbohydrate 70g	23%
Dietary fiber 4g	17%
Sugars 4g	0%
Protein 33g	0%

* Percent daily values are based on a
2,000-calorie diet

For the sauce
◆ 4 tbsp butter
◆ 12 large scallops, cleaned and halved, corals removed if preferred
◆ 8 scallions, trimmed and diagonally sliced
◆ 1 cup snow peas, trimmed and halved

◆ salt and dash of cayenne pepper
◆ scant 1 cup heavy whipping cream

To serve
◆ 1lb fresh angel hair pasta
◆ paprika

Melt the butter in a pan and sauté the scallops for 3 minutes, stirring frequently. Add the scallions and continue to sauté for 1 minute. Add the snow peas and cook for 1 minute. Season to taste. Pour in the cream and let simmer gently while cooking the pasta.

Cook the angel hair pasta in plenty of salted boiling water for 1 minute or until "al dente." Drain and return to the pan. Add the scallop and cream mixture and toss lightly. Serve immediately sprinkled with a little paprika.

ANGEL HAIR PASTA WITH TRUFFLES AND MUSHROOMS

The best truffles are the white ones found in Alba in Piedmont and are available fresh between October to January. Black truffles are found extensively in Umbria and Perigord in France and are used mainly for cooking, as the flavor is not as intense as the white truffle. If white truffle is unavailable, use the black truffle and 1 teaspoon truffle oil.

NUTRITION FACTS

Serving size 1 (217g)
Calories 551   Calories from fat 207

	% daily value *
Total fat 23g	35%
Saturated fat 13g	64%
Monounsaturated fat 5.36g	0%
Polyunsaturated fat 0.77g	0%
Cholesterol 181mg	60%
Sodium 324mg	14%
Total carbohydrate 72g	24%
Dietary fiber 4g	18%
Sugars 3g	0%
Protein 17g	0%

* Percent daily values are based on a
2,000-calorie diet

For the sauce
◆ 1oz dried porcini
◆ 4 tbsp butter
◆ 2-3 smoked or regular garlic cloves, peeled and chopped
◆ 1 onion, peeled and chopped
◆ 3 cups mixed mushrooms, such as field, button, and oyster

◆ 4 tbsp heavy whipping cream
◆ salt and ground black pepper
◆ 1 tbsp chopped fresh flat leaf parsley

To serve
◆ 1lb fresh angel hair pasta
◆ 1oz white truffle, shaved

Soak the porcini in warm water for 30 minutes. Drain and reserve. Heat the butter in a pan and sauté the garlic and onion until softened.

Wipe and roughly chop the mushrooms, then add to the pan with the porcini. Continue to sauté for 5-8 minutes or until the mushrooms have softened. Stir in the cream, seasoning to

taste, and parsley. Heat for 1 minute, then cover with a lid and remove from the heat.

Cook the angel hair pasta in plenty of salted boiling water for 1 minute. Drain well, then return to the pan. Pour over the mushroom sauce. Toss lightly, then serve immediately, sprinkled with the shaved truffle.

Angel Hair Pasta with Scallops

Spaghettini with Leeks and Onions

SPAGHETTINI WITH LEEKS AND ONIONS

I particularly like the flavor of red onions as they have a much sweeter flavor than regular onions. Their color complements the green of the leek.

For the sauce
- 4 tbsp olive oil
- 1 large red onion, peeled and cut into wedges
- 2–3 young leeks, trimmed and sliced
- 4 shallots, peeled and cut into thin slivers
- 2 x 14oz cans chopped tomatoes
- salt and ground black pepper
- 2 tbsp chopped fresh flat leaf parsley

To serve
- 1lb fresh spaghettini
- 4-6 tbsp freshly grated Parmigiano Reggiano

Heat the oil in a skillet and gently sauté the onion for 5 minutes. Add the leeks and shallots and continue to sauté for 3 more minutes. Add the chopped tomatoes with seasoning to taste and simmer gently for 5-8 minutes or until the sauce has been reduced by about half.

Meanwhile, cook the spaghettini in plenty of salted boiling water for 1-2 minutes or until "al dente." Drain thoroughly and return to the pan. Add the sauce to the pan with the chopped parsley and toss lightly. Serve immediately, handing the cheese separately.

NUTRITION FACTS

Serving size 1 (321g)
Calories 559   Calories from fat 207

	% daily value *
Total fat 23g	36%
Saturated fat 5g	23%
Monounsaturated fat 14.4g	0%
Polyunsaturated fat 2.4g	0%
Cholesterol 151mg	50%
Sodium 674mg	28%
Total carbohydrate 70g	23%
Dietary fiber 5g	18%
Sugars 4g	0%
Protein 17g	0%

* Percent daily values are based on a 2,000-calorie diet

FETTUCCINE WITH CHICKEN LIVERS AND MUSHROOMS

Chicken livers are often used in Italian sauces. Here, they have been combined with wild mushrooms to make a particularly tasty dish.

For the sauce
- 1oz dried porcini
- 4 tbsp olive oil
- 2–3 leeks, trimmed and sliced
- 6oz chanterelle mushrooms
- 8oz chicken livers, cleaned and cut into thin strips
- 3 tbsp dry sherry
- 1 tbsp tomato paste
- 5 tbsp chicken stock
- salt and ground black pepper

To serve
- 1lb fresh fettuccine
- freshly shaved Romano cheese

Soak the porcini in warm water for 30 minutes, drain and reserve porcini and liquid.

Heat the oil in a skillet and sauté the leeks for 2 minutes. Add the porcini and chanterelle mushrooms and sauté for 3 minutes. Drain and set to one side.

Add the chicken livers to the pan and quickly seal, stirring. Return the mushrooms to the pan and add the porcini soaking liquid and sherry.

Blend the tomato paste with the stock and seasoning to taste. Stir into the pan. Bring to a boil and simmer for 5 minutes or until a sauce consistency is reached.

Meanwhile, cook the fettuccine in plenty of boiling salted water for 1-2 minutes or until "al dente." Drain and return to the pan. Add the sauce and toss lightly. Serve with the freshly shaved cheese.

NUTRITION FACTS

Serving size 1 (328g)
Calories 637   Calories from fat 207

	% daily value *
Total fat 23g	35%
Saturated fat 5g	26%
Monounsaturated fat 11.3g	0%
Polyunsaturated fat 1.84g	0%
Cholesterol 448mg	149%
Sodium 420mg	18%
Total carbohydrate 80g	27%
Dietary fiber 5g	21%
Sugars 5g	0%
Protein 30g	0%

* Percent daily values are based on a 2,000-calorie diet

TAGLIATELLE WITH MEATBALLS

These tiny meatballs would be ideal to serve with any of the long ribbon pastas.
They would also work equally well with farfalle or fusilli.

NUTRITION FACTS

Serving size 1 (319g)
Calories 689   Calories from fat 261

	% daily value *
Total fat 29g	44%
Saturated fat 9g	44%
Monounsaturated fat 14.1g	0%
Polyunsaturated fat 3.4g	0%
Cholesterol 227mg	76%
Sodium 491mg	20%
Total carbohydrate 75g	25%
Dietary fiber 5g	19%
Sugars 7g	0%
Protein 26g	0%

* Percent daily values are based on a 2,000-calorie diet

For the sauce

◆ 1 small onion, peeled and finely chopped
◆ 1-2 garlic cloves, peeled and minced
◆ 225 g/8 oz lean minced lamb
◆ salt and ground black pepper
◆ 1 tbsp grated lemon rind
◆ ½ cup fresh white bread crumbs
◆ 1 tbsp chopped fresh marjoram
◆ 1 tbsp pine nuts, toasted and chopped
◆ 1 medium egg, beaten

◆ 1-2 tbsp olive oil
◆ 1¼ cups puréed tomatoes
◆ ⅔ cup red wine
◆ few sprigs of marjoram

To serve

◆ 1lb fresh tagliatelle
◆ freshly grated Parmigiano Reggiano
◆ marjoram sprig

Place the onion, garlic, lamb, seasoning, lemon rind, bread crumbs, chopped marjoram, and pine nuts in a bowl and mix well. Bind together with the egg. Dampen your hands, then form the mixture into tiny balls, each about the size of a cherry.

Heat the olive oil in a pan and brown the meatballs on all sides. Remove from the pan and wipe the pan clean. Add the puréed tomatoes, red wine, and marjoram sprigs to the pan and bring to a boil. Boil for 5 minutes, reduce the heat, and add the meatballs. Cover with a lid and simmer gently for 5-8 minutes or until the meatballs are cooked.

Meanwhile, cook the tagliatelle in plenty of salted boiling water for 1-2 minutes or until "al dente." Drain and place on a warm serving platter. Discard the marjoram sprigs from the sauce, then spoon the sauce and meatballs over the tagliatelle. Serve with the grated cheese and garnish with a marjoram sprig.

Tagliatelle with Meatballs

Tagliatelle with Seafood

TAGLIATELLE WITH SEAFOOD

*The choice of fish is entirely up to you, but bear in mind the varying flavors
and textures of the different fish you put together. If you have difficulty obtaining
saffron threads, a tiny dash of turmeric will give the distinctive yellow color but
the flavor will be impaired.*

For the sauce

- 12oz assorted fresh fish fillets, such as salmon, trout, cod, or haddock, skinned
- 4 tbsp butter
- 2 cups thinly sliced leeks
- 1 cup trimmed and sliced button mushrooms
- few strands of saffron
- 5 tbsp dry white wine
- 4 tbsp heavy whipping cream

To serve

- 1lb fresh tagliatelle
- few sprigs of flat leaf parsley

Cut the fish into small cubes, discarding any small bones that may remain after filleting. Heat the butter in a large pan and sauté the leeks and mushrooms for 3 minutes. Add the fish fillets and continue to sauté for 3 more minutes or until sealed. Sprinkle in the saffron, cook for 1 minute, then add the wine. Bring to a boil, cover with a lid, then simmer for 3-4 minutes or until the fish is cooked.

Meanwhile, cook the tagliatelle in plenty of salted boiling water for 3-4 minutes or until "al dente". Drain and return to the pan. Add the fish and cream to the pasta. Toss lightly and garnish with sprigs of flat leaf parsley. Serve immediately.

NUTRITION FACTS

Serving size 1 (319g)
Calories 642   Calories from fat 252

	% daily value *
Total fat 28g	43%
Saturated fat 13g	66%
Monounsaturated fat 9.65g	0%
Polyunsaturated fat 2.44g	0%
Cholesterol 268mg	89%
Sodium 383mg	16%
Total carbohydrate 65g	22%
Dietary fiber 3g	13%
Sugars 4g	0%
Protein 28g	0%

* Percent daily values are based on a 2,000-calorie diet

TRENETTE WITH ARUGULA AND RADICCHIO

*Many of us have only recently discovered the delights of both arugula and radicchio,
but they are ingredients that are used regularly in many Italian dishes.*

For the sauce

- 4 tbsp olive oil
- 4 shallots, peeled and sliced
- 4oz prosciutto, thinly sliced into strips
- 14oz can artichoke hearts, drained and quartered
- 3 tbsp vegetable stock
- 1 small head radicchio, thinly sliced
- salt and ground black pepper
- 1 tbsp balsamic vinegar
- 1 small bunch arugula

To serve

- 1lb fresh trenette

Heat the oil in a pan and sauté the shallots and prosciutto for 5 minutes or until softened. Add the artichoke hearts, then stir in the stock and bring to a boil. Simmer for 2 minutes or until the liquid has reduced slightly.

Add the radicchio and simmer for 3 minutes or until the radicchio has softened. Season to taste. Cover with a lid and remove from the heat.

Meanwhile, cook the trenette in plenty of salted boiling water for 1-2 minutes or until "al dente." Drain and return to the pan. Add the radicchio mixture to the pan together with the balsamic vinegar and arugula. Toss lightly and serve immediately.

NUTRITION FACTS

Serving size 1 (206g)
Calories 555   Calories from fat 243

	% daily value *
Total fat 27g	42%
Saturated fat 6g	28%
Monounsaturated fat 16.5g	0%
Polyunsaturated fat 2.90g	0%
Cholesterol 166mg	55%
Sodium 807mg	34%
Total carbohydrate 59g	20%
Dietary fiber 2g	9%
Sugars 3g	0%
Protein 18g	0%

* Percent daily values are based on a 2,000-calorie diet

CHAPTER SIX

FILLED PASTA

This chapter features classic dishes such as cannelloni, lasagna, and ravioli. There are endless combinations that can be used with these pastas and whether it is fish, meat, or vegetables, all of them are served with a sauce. Remember that the sauce needs to complement the pasta, not overwhelm its taste and texture.

WHOLEWHEAT LASAGNA WITH MEDITERRANEAN VEGETABLES

With the greater emphasis on healthy eating, more people are adopting the Mediterranean way of eating. With their vast array of sun-ripened vegetables, delicious pastas, breads, and rich unctuous oils, it is easy to see why. Try this recipe, which captures this richness.

- 3 tbsp olive oil
- 1 onion, peeled and chopped
- 3 garlic cloves, peeled and minced
- 6 sun-dried tomatoes, chopped
- 2 cups chopped eggplant
- 1 yellow bell pepper, seeded and chopped
- 1 red bell pepper, seeded and chopped
- 2 cups chopped zucchini
- 2 cups puréed tomatoes
- ⅔ cup red wine
- salt and ground black pepper
- 1 tbsp chopped fresh oregano
- 6-8 fresh wholewheat lasagna sheets
- 4 firm tomatoes, sliced
- ½ cup grated mozzarella cheese
- extra chopped fresh oregano

Preheat the oven to 375°F, 10 minutes before baking the lasagna. Heat the oil in a skillet and sauté the onion, garlic, and sun-dried tomatoes for 5 minutes. Add the eggplant, yellow and red peppers, and zucchini, and continue to sauté for 3 more minutes.

Stir in the puréed tomatoes, wine, seasoning to taste, and the oregano. Bring to a boil, reduce the heat, and simmer for 15 minutes or until the vegetables are almost cooked.

Bring a large pan of water to a boil, add 1 tablespoon salt, then drop in four lasagna sheets, one at a time. Cook for 2-3 minutes, ensuring that they do not stick together. Drain, lay them on clean dish towels, and pat dry. Repeat with the remaining lasagna sheets.

Place a layer of the vegetable sauce in the base of an ovenproof dish and top with half the lasagna sheets. Cover with the remaining sauce and then the lasagna sheets.

Arrange the tomato slices on top and sprinkle with the grated cheese. Bake in the oven for 25 minutes or until the cheese is golden and brown. Serve sprinkled with chopped oregano.

NUTRITION FACTS

Serving size 1 (585g)
Calories 517   Calories from fat 135

	% daily value *
Total fat 15g	23%
Saturated fat 3g	17%
Monounsaturated fat 7.7g	0%
Polyunsaturated fat 1.4g	0%
Cholesterol 8mg	2%
Sodium 299mg	12%
Total carbohydrate 80g	27%
Dietary fiber 8g	32%
Sugars 11g	0%
Protein 20g	0%

* Percent daily values are based on a 2,000-calorie diet

SEAFOOD LASAGNA

Traditionally, everyone thinks of lasagna with a ragu sauce, but in my opinion this version is one of the most delicious of all pasta recipes. You can vary the fish used according to availability and personal choice.

- 8oz white fish fillets, such as cod
- 8oz smoked haddock fillet or similar smoked fish
- 2½ cups skim milk
- 2-3 bay leaves
- 1 small onion, sliced
- few sprigs of parsley
- 4 tbsp butter or margarine
- ½ cup all-purpose flour
- 1 tsp wholegrain mustard
- ¼ cup grated hard cheese, such as aged Cheddar or Gruyère
- salt and ground black pepper
- 1 cup shelled shrimp, thawed if frozen
- 1 cup tiny broccoli flowerets, blanched
- 6-8 fresh lasagna sheets
- 4 firm tomatoes, sliced
- ¼ cup freshly grated Parmesan cheese

Preheat the oven to 375°F, 10 minutes before baking the lasagna. Wipe the fish and skin, discarding any bones. Place in a skillet with 1¼ cups of the milk, the bay leaves, onion, and parsley. Place over a gentle heat and bring to a boil. Simmer for 8 minutes or until the fish is just cooked. Drain, reserving the milk; flake the fish and reserve.

For the white sauce, melt the butter or margarine in a small pan and stir in the flour. Cook, stirring, for 2 minutes. Remove from the heat and gradually stir in both amounts of reserved milk. Return to the heat and cook, stirring throughout, until the sauce thickens. Remove from the heat and stir in the mustard, grated cheese, and seasoning to taste. Stir until the cheese has melted.

Squeeze out any excess moisture from the shrimp and add to the flaked fish with the blanched broccoli.

Bring a large pan of water to a boil, add 1 tablespoon salt, then drop in four lasagna sheets, one at a time. Cook for 2-3 minutes, ensuring that they do not stick together. Drain, lay them on clean dish towels, and pat dry. Repeat with the remaining lasagna sheets.

Spoon about a quarter of the prepared sauce into the base of an ovenproof dish and top with 3-4 sheets of lasagna. Cover this with half the fish and broccoli mixture and spoon over a further quarter of the sauce.

Repeat the layers, finishing with the lasagna sheets. Arrange the sliced tomatoes on top. Spoon over the remaining sauce and sprinkle with the grated Parmesan cheese. Bake the lasagna in the oven for 25 minutes or until golden brown and bubbly.

Seafood Lasagna

HAM, TOMATO, AND MOZZARELLA RAVIOLI

The combinations for ravioli are endless, so instead of using the traditional meat filling, experiment with your favorite ingredients.

- ½ cup ricotta cheese
- 2 cups mozzarella cheese, thinly sliced
- 4oz smoked ham, thinly sliced and cut into thin strips
- 2 firm tomatoes, peeled, seeded, and chopped
- salt and ground black pepper
- 1 tbsp wholegrain mustard
- batch basic pasta dough (see page 20)
- 4 tbsp butter
- 1 tbsp chopped fresh sage

Place cheeses, smoked ham, tomatoes, seasoning, and 1 teaspoon of the mustard in a mixing bowl, mix well, and reserve.

Roll the pasta dough out and proceed to make the ravioli as previously described (see page 24). Repeat until all the filling and pasta has been used. Let dry 1 hour before separating the squares.

Cook the ravioli in plenty of salted boiling water for 4-5 minutes or until "al dente." Drain and return to the pan. Add the remaining mustard, the butter, and sage, and toss lightly until the butter has melted and the ravioli is lightly coated. Serve immediately.

SPINACH, MUSHROOM, AND RICOTTA CANNELLONI

The combination of spinach and ricotta cheese is superb and this filling would work equally well for either ravioli or lasagna.

- 1 tbsp olive oil
- 1 small onion, peeled and finely chopped
- ¾ cup finely chopped mushrooms
- 1 cup ricotta cheese
- 1 cup thawed frozen spinach
- salt and ground black pepper
- ½-1 tsp freshly grated nutmeg
- 12-14 fresh lasagna sheets
- Quick Tomato Sauce (see page 36)
- ½ cup grated mozzarella cheese

Preheat the oven to 375°F, 10 minutes before baking the cannelloni. Heat the oil in a small pan and sauté the onion and mushrooms for 5 minutes. Drain and reserve.

Beat the ricotta cheese until soft and creamy, then beat in the drained onion mixture. Squeeze out any excess moisture from the spinach and beat into the cheese mixture together with seasoning to taste and the grated nutmeg.

Bring a large pan of water to a boil, add 1 tablespoon salt then drop in four lasagna sheets, one at a time. Cook for 1-2 minutes,

ensuring that they do not stick together. Drain, lay them on clean dish towels, and pat dry. Repeat with the remaining lasagna sheets.

Place about 2 tablespoons of the prepared filling at one end of a lasagna sheet. Moisten the edges and roll up to encase the filling. Dampen the edge to seal.

Place the filled tubes, seam side down, into the base of an ovenproof dish. Pour over the Quick Tomato Sauce. Sprinkle with the cheese. Bake the cannelloni in the oven for 25 minutes or until golden and bubbly.

VEGETABLE LASAGNA

There are many different fillings that can be used for lasagna. With the abundance of vegetables so readily available it would not be difficult to create a different lasagna for every day of the week.

- 4 tbsp butter or margarine
- ½ cup all-purpose flour
- 2½ cups milk
- salt and ground black pepper
- 1½ cups carrots, peeled and sliced into half moon shapes
- 1 cup shelled fava beans
- 1 cup green beans, trimmed and cut into 2-inch lengths
- 1 cup baby cauliflower flowerets
- 14oz can red kidney beans, drained and rinsed
- ¾ cup chopped, thawed frozen spinach
- ½ cup grated Cheddar cheese
- 1 tsp wholegrain mustard
- 6-8 fresh lasagna sheets
- 4 firm tomatoes, sliced
- 3 medium eggs
- ⅔ cup thick yogurt

NUTRITION FACTS

Serving size 1 (849g)
Calories 1058   Calories from fat 288

	% daily value *
Total fat 32g	49%
Saturated fat 16g	82%
Monounsaturated fat 8.21g	0%
Polyunsaturated fat 1.99g	0%
Cholesterol 235mg	78%
Sodium 694mg	29%
Total carbohydrate 150g	50%
Dietary fiber 18g	73%
Sugars 21g	0%
Protein 48g	0%

* Percent daily values are based on a 2,000-calorie diet

Preheat the oven to 375°F, 10 minutes before baking the lasagna. Melt the butter or margarine in a small pan and stir in the flour. Cook over a gentle heat for 2 minutes then draw off the heat and gradually stir in the milk. Return the pan to the heat and cook, stirring until smooth, thick, and glossy. Season and remove the pan from the heat. Cover with a sheet of dampened wax paper and reserve.

Cook the carrots in lightly salted boiling water for 5 minutes or until just tender. Drain and reserve. Blanch the fava beans, green beans, and cauliflower for 3 minutes. Drain and refresh in cold water. Mix with the carrots and kidney beans.

Squeeze out any excess moisture from the spinach, then beat into the prepared white sauce with the cheese, seasoning to taste, and the mustard. Place over a gentle heat and stir until smooth.

Bring a large pan of water to a boil, add 1 tablespoon salt, then drop in four lasagna sheets, one at a time. Cook for 2-3 minutes, ensuring that they do not stick together. Drain, lay them on clean dish towels, and pat dry. Repeat with the remaining lasagna sheets.

Place half the sauce and vegetables in the base of an ovenproof dish and cover with 3-4 lasagna sheets. Repeat once more, finishing with the pasta. Arrange the tomato slices on top. Beat the eggs with the yogurt, then pour over the tomatoes.

Bake the lasagna in the oven for 25-30 minutes or until the top is golden brown and bubbly. Serve.

Tortelloni with Parma Ham

TORTELLONI WITH PARMA HAM

Tortelloni take a little time and practice to make, but do persevere as they are well worth that extra bit of effort and are far superior to store-bought ones. To begin with, use a simple sauce as used here, then as you get more proficient you can try different sauce and filling combinations.

- 1-2 tsp butter
- 2 small onions, peeled and finely chopped
- ½ cup finely chopped mushrooms
- 1 cup ricotta cheese
- ½ cup grated Gruyère cheese
- 4oz Parma ham, trimmed and finely shredded
- batch basic pasta dough (see page 20)

- 1 tsp olive oil
- 4 scallions, trimmed and finely chopped
- 14oz can chopped tomatoes
- salt and ground black pepper
- 2 tbsp chopped fresh flat leaf parsley
- freshly grated Parmesan cheese

For the filling, melt the butter in a small pan and gently sauté one onion for 3 minutes. Add the mushrooms and continue to sauté for a further 3 minutes or until the mushrooms are lightly cooked. Drain and reserve.

Beat the ricotta cheese until creamy. Beat in the Gruyère cheese, the drained mushrooms, and ham. Mix together.

Make the dough and roll out into long, thin sheets about 4-inches wide (see page 22).

Place the filling in a large pastry bag and pipe small rounds of the filling onto one half of the dough. Brush the dough with a little water and fold over to completely encase the filling.

Cut into squares using a fluted cookie cutter, making sure each square contains filling.

Moisten the edges and fold each square in half to form a triangle, pinching the edges together.

Pull the two corners together, wrapping them round the tip of your finger. Pinch the corners together on the seam. Repeat until all the triangles have been formed.

Cook the tortelloni in plenty of salted boiling water for 4-5 minutes. Drain and transfer to a serving dish.

While cooking the tortelloni, make the sauce. Heat the oil and gently sauté the other onion and scallions for 2 minutes. Add the contents of the can of tomatoes and simmer for 5 minutes. Add seasoning to taste and the chopped parsley. Pour over the cooked tortelloni and serve with grated Parmesan cheese.

NUTRITION FACTS

Serving size 1 (389g)
Calories 626   Calories from fat 225

	% daily value *
Total fat 25g	39%
Saturated fat 11g	57%
Monounsaturated fat 9.52g	0%
Polyunsaturated fat 1.89g	0%
Cholesterol 214mg	71%
Sodium 1259mg	52%
Total carbohydrate 65g	22%
Dietary fiber 4g	14%
Sugars 5g	0%
Protein 32g	0%

* Percent daily values are based on a 2,000-calorie diet

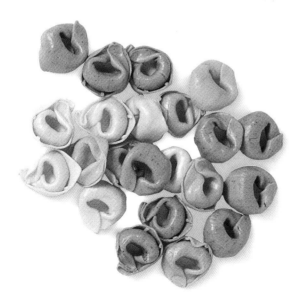

EASY-OVER RAVIOLI

This recipe takes the idea of ravioli but it is designed for those of us who have hectic lives. You can try the recipe with a variety of fillings. I have used ground chicken, but it would work equally well with ground lamb, beef, or pork.

NUTRITION FACTS

Serving size 1 (321g)
Calories 836   Calories from fat 315

	% daily value *
Total fat 35g	54%
Saturated fat 9g	47%
Monounsaturated fat 16.2g	0%
Polyunsaturated fat 4.39g	0%
Cholesterol 282mg	94%
Sodium 615mg	26%
Total carbohydrate 98g	33%
Dietary fiber 6g	23%
Sugars 8g	0%
Protein 32g	0%

* Percent daily values are based on a 2,000-calorie diet

- 2 tbsp olive oil
- 1 jalapeño chile, seeded and finely chopped
- 6 scallions, trimmed and finely chopped
- 8oz ground chicken
- ¼ cup ready-to-eat dried apricots finely chopped
- ¼ cup toasted and chopped pine nuts
- 1 cup fresh white bread crumbs
- 1 medium egg, beaten
- batch basic pasta dough (see page 20)
- Spicy Tomato Sauce (see page 29)
- few sprigs flat leaf parsley

Heat 1 tablespoon oil in a pan and sauté the chile for 2 minutes. Add the scallions and sauté for 1 more minute.

Add the chicken and sauté for 5 minutes or until cooked. Stir in the apricots, pine nuts, and bread crumbs, mixing well. Remove from the heat and add the egg to the mixture. Bind together. Return to the heat and cook gently for 2 minutes or until completely cooked. Keep warm.

Meanwhile, roll out the pasta dough and cut into 3-inch squares. Bring a large pan of water to a boil and add 1 tablespoon oil. Add the pasta squares, one at a time, and cook for about 3-4 minutes. Carefully remove and keep warm between clean, warm dish towels.

Reheat the tomato sauce, stirring occasionally. Place 2-3 cooked pasta squares onto warm plates. Top with a spoonful or two of the chicken mixture and cover with a further layer of pasta. Drizzle over a little tomato sauce and hand the remaining sauce separately. Garnish with flat leaf parsley sprigs.

TORTELLONI WITH RICOTTA AND HERBS

You can vary the herbs you use according to personal preference and availability. If liked, you can also use chopped spinach or even arugula.

NUTRITION FACTS

Serving size 1 (216g)
Calories 534   Calories from fat 198

	% daily value *
Total fat 22g	34%
Saturated fat 10g	52%
Monounsaturated fat 7.85g	0%
Polyunsaturated fat 1.72g	0%
Cholesterol 248mg	83%
Sodium 1965mg	82%
Total carbohydrate 59g	20%
Dietary fiber 2g	9%
Sugars 2g	0%
Protein 24g	0%

* Percent daily values are based on a 2,000-calorie diet

- 1 cup ricotta
- ½ cup finely chopped fontina
- 4 tbsp chopped fresh mixed herbs, such as basil, sage, flat leaf parsley, and oregano
- 1 medium egg yolk
- salt and ground black pepper
- ½ tsp grated nutmeg
- batch basic pasta dough (see page 20)
- Butter and Tomato Sauce (see page 39)
- freshly grated Parmigiano Reggiano cheese
- extra 2 tbsp chopped fresh herbs to serve

For the filling, mix the cheeses with the 4 tablespoons chopped herbs, egg yolk, seasoning, and nutmeg in a bowl. Roll out the pasta to 4-inch wide strips.

Place the filling in a pastry bag and pipe small rounds onto one half of each strip. Moisten the edges and fold the dough over to completely encase the filling. Cut out into squares and proceed to form the tortelloni as previously described on page 83.

Cook the tortelloni in plenty of salted boiling water for 4-5 minutes or until "al dente." Drain and return to the pan.

Gently heat the sauce then pour over the cooked tortelloni. Toss lightly until coated. Serve immediately, sprinkled with extra chopped herbs and handing some grated Parmigiano Reggiano cheese separately.

Easy-over Ravioli

Turkey, Tomato, and Basil Lasagna

Use finely chopped turkey breast, or if preferred, chopped or ground chicken breast to make this tasty lasagna.

- 2 tbsp olive oil
- 1 large onion, peeled and finely chopped
- 2-3 garlic cloves, peeled and minced
- 12oz ground turkey
- 2 x 14oz cans chopped tomatoes
- salt and ground black pepper
- 2 tbsp chopped fresh basil
- 6-8 fresh lasagna verdi sheets
- 2 cups zucchini, peeled, sliced lengthways, and blanched
- ½ cup grated mozzarella cheese
- fresh basil sprigs

Preheat the oven to 375°F, 10 minutes before baking the lasagna. Heat the oil in a large pan and sauté the onion and garlic for 5 minutes or until the onion is softened. Add the ground turkey and continue to sauté for a further 5 minutes or until sealed.

Add the contents of the cans of tomatoes, bring to a boil, then reduce the heat and simmer for 10 minutes or until a thick consistency is formed. Season to taste and stir in the basil.

Bring a large pan of water to a boil, add 1 tablespoon salt, then drop in four lasagna sheets, one at a time. Cook for 2-3 minutes, ensuring that they do not stick together. Drain, lay them on clean dish towels, and pat dry. Repeat with the remaining lasagna sheets.

Place about a third of the sauce in the base of an ovenproof dish and cover with a layer of blanched zucchini slices, then 3-4 lasagna sheets. Repeat the layering, finishing with a layer of sauce. Sprinkle with the grated cheese. Bake the lasagna in the oven for 20-25 minutes or until the cheese is golden. Serve garnished with fresh basil sprigs.

Ravioli with Mixed Mushrooms

A good flavored tomato sauce is an ideal choice to serve with this ravioli, with a final sprinkling of freshly grated Parmesan cheese to serve.

- 3 tbsp butter
- 2 small onions, peeled and finely chopped
- 2 cups finely chopped mixed mushrooms
- ½ cup ricotta cheese
- salt and ground black pepper
- batch basic pasta dough (see page 20)
- 1¼ cups puréed tomatoes
- 2 tbsp chopped fresh basil
- freshly grated Parmigiano Reggiano

For the filling, heat 2 tablespoons butter in a small pan and gently sauté one onion for 5 minutes. Add the mushrooms and sauté for a further 5 minutes, stirring frequently. Remove from the heat and let cool.

Beat the ricotta until smooth. Mix in the cooled mushrooms with seasoning to taste. Roll out the pasta dough and proceed to make the ravioli as shown on page 24.

For the sauce, melt the remaining butter in a pan and sauté the onion for 5 minutes. Add the puréed tomatoes and simmer for 10 minutes. Season to taste and add the basil.

Cook the ravioli in plenty of salted boiling water for 4-5 minutes or until "al dente" and drain. Return to the pan. Add the sauce and toss the cooked ravioli lightly until coated. Serve with the grated cheese.

Turkey, Tomato, and Basil Lasagna

Salmon and Asparagus Ravioli

SALMON AND ASPARAGUS RAVIOLI

This recipe uses smoked salmon; however, it works very well with fresh salmon. If using fresh salmon, ensure that all the bones are removed before using.

- 4–5 asparagus spears, tough stems discarded
- ¾ cup ricotta cheese
- 4oz smoked salmon, cut into thin strips
- 2 tsp grated lemon rind
- ground black pepper
- batch basic pasta dough (see page 20)
- ⅓ cup sour cream
- 1 tbsp chopped fresh dill

Blanch the asparagus in boiling water for 2 minutes; drain. Blend the ricotta cheese and smoked salmon together in a bowl. Finely chop the blanched asparagus and stir into the smoked salmon mixture, together with the lemon rind and black pepper. Reserve.

Roll out the pasta dough and proceed to make the ravioli as previously described on page 24, placing the prepared filling in the hopper as before.

Cook the ravioli in salted boiling water for 4-5 minutes or until "al dente." Drain and return to the pan. Add the sour cream and dill. Heat through, gently stirring, for 2 minutes, then serve immediately.

NUTRITION FACTS

Serving size 1 (253g)
Calories 547   Calories from fat 207

	% daily value *
Total fat 23g	35%
Saturated fat 11g	54%
Monounsaturated fat 8.45g	0%
Polyunsaturated fat 1.85g	0%
Cholesterol 193mg	64%
Sodium 475mg	20%
Total carbohydrate 59g	20%
Dietary fiber 2g	10%
Sugars 3g	0%
Protein 24g	0%

* Percent daily values are based on a 2,000-calorie diet

PASTA ROULADE

This dish takes a little while to prepare but the finished result is well worth all the effort. You can vary the filling; try adding ½ cup chopped wild mushrooms or add some chopped prosciutto and peeled, seeded, chopped tomatoes.

- 2 tbsp butter
- 1 onion, peeled and chopped
- 2 garlic cloves, peeled and minced
- 1¼ cups thawed frozen spinach. chopped
- 1½ cups mushrooms, wiped and finely chopped
- ¾ cup goat cheese, crumbled
- ¾ cup ricotta cheese
- salt and ground black pepper
- ½ tsp grated nutmeg
- 8oz basic pasta dough (see page 20)
- 1 cup vegetable stock
- 1¾ cups Quick Tomato Sauce (see page 36)
- sprigs of basil

Preheat the oven to 375°F, 10 minutes before baking the pasta. For filling, melt the butter in a heavy pan and sauté the onion and garlic for 2 minutes. Squeeze out any excess moisture from the spinach. Add to the pan with the mushrooms and cook gently for 2 minutes. Stir in the goat cheese and ricotta with the seasoning to taste and nutmeg.

Using your pasta machine, roll out the pasta into 5-inch wide strips. Cut into 4-inch lengths. Cook the pasta sheets in plenty of salted boiling water, a few at a time, for 3-4 minutes. Stir occasionally to prevent the sheets sticking.

Remove the strips from the pan and drain thoroughly on clean dish towels.

Spread the pasta sheets with the filling and roll them up to encase it. Place in a buttered ovenproof dish. Pour the vegetable stock over the pasta, cover with aluminum foil, and cook in the preheated oven for 20 minutes or until piping hot.

Meanwhile, reheat the prepared sauce. To serve, spoon a little of the prepared sauce onto each serving plate. Arrange 3-4 pasta rolls on top of the sauce. Garnish with the basil sprigs and serve immediately.

NUTRITION FACTS

Serving size 1 (479g)
Calories 814   Calories from fat 351

	% daily value *
Total fat 39g	59%
Saturated fat 18g	90%
Monounsaturated fat 13.8g	0%
Polyunsaturated fat 3.02g	0%
Cholesterol 480mg	160%
Sodium 1125mg	47%
Total carbohydrate 78g	26%
Dietary fiber 5g	20%
Sugars 4g	0%
Protein 39g	0%

* Percent daily values are based on a 2,000-calorie diet

CRAB AND SCALLION CANNELLONI

If you are fortunate enough to live in an area where freshly caught crabs are obtainable, this recipe is a must for you. However, it is possible to use canned or even frozen crab meat; just ensure that you gently squeeze out any excess moisture.

- 10oz white crab meat
- 6 scallions, trimmed and finely chopped
- 2-3 small jalapeño chiles, seeded and finely chopped
- 3 firm tomatoes, peeled, seeded, and finely chopped
- salt and ground black pepper
- 10-12 fresh lasagna sheets
- 1 tbsp olive oil
- 1 medium onion, peeled and finely chopped
- 14oz can chopped tomatoes
- ⅔ cup puréed tomatoes
- ½ cup grated Gruyère cheese
- sprigs of flat leaf parsley

Preheat the oven to 375°F, 10 minutes before baking the cannelloni. Place the crab meat, scallions, chopped chiles, and tomatoes with seasoning to taste in a bowl and mix together.

Bring a large pan of water to a boil, add 1 tablespoon salt, then drop in four lasagna sheets, one at a time. Cook for 2-3 minutes, ensuring that they do not stick together. Drain, lay them on clean dish towels, and pat dry. Repeat with the remaining lasagna sheets.

Place about 2 tablespoons crab mixture at one end of a lasagna sheet. Moisten the edges and roll up to encase the filling. Dampen the edge to seal. Place the filled tubes, seam side down, into the base of an ovenproof dish.

Heat the oil in a skillet and sauté the onion for 5 minutes. Add the contents of the can of tomatoes and the puréed tomatoes, and bring to a boil. Reduce the heat and simmer for 10 minutes. Season to taste.

Pour the sauce over the filled tubes and sprinkle with the cheese. Bake the cannelloni in the oven for 25 minutes or until golden. Garnish with fresh flat leaf parsley sprigs.

TORTELLONI WITH SHRIMP

When making stuffed pastas it is important to ensure that your pasta does not dry out while you are filling it. It is best to keep the dough you are not working with tightly covered in plastic wrap.

- ⅔ cup freshly grated Parmigiano Reggiano
- 4oz shelled shrimp
- 8oz white fish fillets, skinned and boned
- 1 medium egg yolk
- 2 tbsp heavy whipping cream
- salt and ground black pepper
- 1 tsp anchovy extract
- batch basic pasta dough (see page 20)
- 3 tbsp olive oil
- 4 shallots, peeled and finely chopped
- 1 tbsp tomato paste
- 4 tbsp dry white wine
- ⅔ cup sour cream
- 1 tbsp chopped fresh dill

For the filling, place the cheese, shrimp, fish, and egg yolk in a food processor. Blend, adding sufficient cream to form a thick filling. Season to taste and add the anchovy extract.

Roll out the pasta dough into 3-inch strips and use the prepared filling to make the tortelloni as previously described on page 83. Cook the tortelloni in plenty of salted boiling water for 4-5 minutes or until "al dente." Drain and return to the pan.

Meanwhile, for the sauce, heat the oil in a pan and sauté the shallots for 3 minutes. Blend the tomato paste with the wine and stir into the pan. Bring to a boil and simmer for 3 minutes.

Stir in the sour cream and dill, then heat for 1 minute. Pour over the pasta, toss, and serve.

Crab and Scallion Cannelloni

BEEF AND MUSHROOM CANNELLONI

In this recipe I have used porcini and chanterelle mushrooms, but if you prefer, you can use regular mushrooms.

- 1 cup milk
- ½ small onion, peeled
- small piece carrot, peeled
- 1 celery stick, trimmed
- 2-3 whole cloves
- few black peppercorns
- 1-2 bayleaves
- few parsley stalks
- 2 tbsp butter or margarine
- ¼ cup all-purpose flour
- salt

- ½oz dried porcini, soaked in warm water for 30 minutes
- 8oz lean ground beef
- 1 onion, peeled and finely chopped
- 2 garlic cloves, peeled and minced
- ¾ cup finely chopped chanterelle mushrooms
- ⅔ cup red wine
- 2 tbsp tomato paste
- ground black pepper
- 12 fresh lasagna sheets
- ¾ cup sliced mozzarella cheese

Preheat the oven to 375°F, 10 minutes before baking the cannelloni. Pour the milk into a small saucepan and add the onion, carrot, celery, cloves, peppercorns, bayleaves, and parsley stalks. Slowly bring the milk to just below boiling point then remove from the heat, cover, and leave to infuse for at least 15 minutes. Strain, reserving the milk.

Melt the butter or margarine in a small pan and stir in the flour. Cook over a gentle heat for 2 minutes then draw off the heat and gradually stir in the reserved milk. Return pan to the heat and cook, stirring until smooth, thick, and glossy. Season with the salt. Cover with a sheet of dampened waxed paper and reserve.

Drain the porcini, reserving the liquor, and chop. Sauté the beef in a skillet until browned, stirring frequently to help to break up any lumps. Add the onion, garlic, porcini, and chanterelles, and continue to sauté for 5 minutes or until the onion is softened.

Pour in the wine, bring to a boil, and simmer for 5 minutes. Blend the tomato paste with the reserved porcini soaking water and 2 tablespoons of water. Stir into the beef mixture with black pepper to taste. Cook for 5 more minutes. Remove from the heat and cool.

Bring a large pan of water to a boil, add 1 tablespoon of salt, then drop in four lasagna sheets, one at a time. Cook for 2-3 minutes, ensuring that they do not stick together. Drain, lay them on clean dish towels, and pat dry. Repeat with the remaining lasagna sheets.

Use the prepared beef mixture to fill the pasta sheets and roll up (see page 90). Place in the base of an ovenproof dish. Top with the prepared sauce and dot with the cheese slices. Bake the cannelloni in the oven for 25 minutes or until golden and bubbly. Serve immediately.

CHAPTER SEVEN

COLORED AND FLAVORED PASTAS

With the wide array of colored, flavored pastas it is possible to make, no pasta book would be complete without a complete chapter devoted to them. From black to saffron, red to green, there is absolutely no limit to the color combinations that can be achieved, especially if you take into account the sauces and herbs that can be used as well.

TOMATO SPAGHETTI WITH MUSHROOMS

For this dish you need to include at least one kind of dried mushroom as this will give the depth of flavor that is so synonymous with all Italian mushroom-based dishes. Dried porcini keep so well, they are an ingredient that no well-stocked kitchen should be without.

For the sauce
- ½oz dried porcini
- 3 tbsp olive oil
- 1 red onion, peeled and cut into wedges
- 3-6 smoked or regular garlic cloves, peeled and thinly sliced
- 1½ cups mushrooms, such as oyster or chanterelle, wiped and sliced
- 1½ cups button mushrooms, wiped and sliced

- 6 tbsp red wine
- 2 tbsp extra virgin olive oil
- salt and ground black pepper
- 2 tbsp chopped fresh sage

To serve
- 1lb fresh tomato spaghetti
- fresh chopped sage leaves

Soak the porcini in warm water for about 30 minutes. Drain, reserving the soaking liquid, and chop the porcini.

Heat the oil in a pan and sauté the onion and garlic for 3 minutes. Add the chopped porcini, oyster or chanterelle, and button mushrooms. Sauté for a further 5 minutes, stirring frequently.

Strain the porcini soaking liquid into the pan and add the red wine. Bring to a boil, then simmer for 5 minutes or until the mushrooms are just cooked and the liquid has been reduced by about half. Stir in the extra virgin olive oil, seasoning to taste, and sage. Cover with lid, remove from the heat, and reserve.

Meanwhile, cook the tomato spaghetti in plenty of salted boiling water for 1-2 minutes or until "al dente." Drain and return to the pan. Add the mushrooms and sauce and toss ingredients lightly. Serve, garnished with the fresh chopped sage leaves.

BEET AND CHEESE RAVIOLI

I am a great fan of beet and cheese; the combination, to my mind, has no equal. Try this exciting combination and taste for yourself.

- 1 cup ricotta cheese
- ½ cup grated Gruyère cheese
- 2 tbsp snipped fresh chives
- 1 medium egg yolk

- salt and ground black pepper
- batch beet pasta dough
- ⅔ cup plain yogurt
- freshly snipped chives

Blend the ricotta, Gruyère cheese, chives, egg yolk, and seasoning together in a bowl until smooth. Reserve.

Roll the pasta dough out and proceed to make the ravioli as previously described on page 24. Once one sheet of dough has been filled, repeat until all the dough and filling has been used. Let the ravioli dry on clean dish towels for 1 hour before cooking.

Cook the ravioli in plenty of salted boiling water for 4-5 minutes or until "al dente." Drain and return to the pan. Add the yogurt and stir lightly. Sprinkle with the snipped chives and serve immediately.

Tomato Spaghetti with Mushrooms

Black Tagliolini with Leeks and Orange

BLACK TAGLIOLINI WITH LEEKS AND ORANGE

Serve this colorful and attractive dish scattered with lashings of freshly shaved Romano cheese, a tossed green salad, and plenty of Italian crusty bread.

For the sauce
- 2 tbsp butter
- 2 cups sliced small leeks
- 1½ cups halved canned baby corn
- grated rind and juice of 1 large orange
- 1 large orange, cut into sections
- ¼ cup roughly chopped pecan halves

- 4 tbsp dry white wine
- salt and ground black pepper

To serve
- 1 lb fresh black tagliolini
- freshly shaved Romano cheese

Melt the butter in a pan and sauté the leeks for 3 minutes or until just beginning to soften. Add the corn, orange rind, and juice, and heat through for 2-3 minutes. Add the orange pieces with the chopped pecan halves, wine, and seasoning to taste. Cover with a lid, remove from the heat, and reserve.

Meanwhile, cook the black tagliolini in plenty of salted boiling water for 1-2 minutes or until "al dente." Drain and return to the pan. Add the leek and orange sauce, toss lightly, then serve sprinkled with the shaved Romano cheese.

NUTRITION FACTS

Serving size 1 (330g)
Calories 574   Calories from fat 189

	% daily value *
Total fat 21g	32%
Saturated fat 7g	36%
Monounsaturated fat 9.23g	0%
Polyunsaturated fat 2.82g	0%
Cholesterol 169mg	56%
Sodium 683mg	28%
Total carbohydrate 78g	26%
Dietary fiber 6g	23%
Sugars 12g	0%
Protein 18g	0%

* Percent daily values are based on a 2,000-calorie diet

LASAGNA VERDI WITH MUSHROOMS AND RAGU SAUCE

This is a dish that is ideal for freezing, so when you have plenty of time, make this, then freeze it ready for use at a later date. Use any mix of mushrooms you like. You can sprinkle the yogurt topping with some grated mozzarella cheese.

- 3 tbsp olive oil
- 4 cups sliced mixed mushrooms
- Ragu Sauce (see page 38)

- 6-8 fresh lasagna verdi sheets
- 2 medium eggs
- ⅔ cup thick, unflavored yogurt

Preheat the oven to 375°F, 10 minutes before baking the lasagna. Heat the oil in a pan and gently sauté the mushrooms for 5 minutes, stirring occasionally, until softened. Remove from the heat and drain. Warm the ragu sauce if made previously and stir well.

Bring a large pan of water to a boil, add 1 tablespoon salt, then drop in four lasagna sheets, one at a time. Cook for 2-3 minutes, ensuring that they do not stick together. Drain and lay them on clean dish towels and pat dry. Repeat with the remaining lasagna sheets.

Place a layer of the ragu sauce in the base of an ovenproof dish and cover with 3-4 sheets of lasagna. Cover the lasagna with half the cooked mushrooms and top with the remaining ragu sauce. Cover with remaining lasagna sheets, then the rest of the mushrooms.

Beat the eggs with the yogurt and pour over the mushrooms. Cook the lasagna in the oven for 30 minutes or until golden.

NUTRITION FACTS

Serving size 1 (413g)
Calories 631   Calories from fat 171

	% daily value *
Total fat 19g	29%
Saturated fat 4g	19%
Monounsaturated fat 9.27g	0%
Polyunsaturated fat 1.22g	0%
Cholesterol 89mg	30%
Sodium 326mg	14%
Total carbohydrate 94g	31%
Dietary fiber 6g	25%
Sugars 8g	0%
Protein 24g	0%

* Percent daily values are based on a 2,000-calorie diet

WHOLEWHEAT SPAGHETTINI WITH AVOCADO

Most people never think of cooking with avocados; this is a shame as their creamy texture makes an ideal sauce when puréed. Their flesh also works well if used when still reasonably firm and added to pasta or stir fry at the end of the cooking time.

For the sauce

◆ 1 ripe avocado and 1 slightly firmer avocado
◆ 2 tbsp lemon juice
◆ 3 tbsp olive oil
◆ 4 plum tomatoes, peeled, seeded, and sliced
◆ 1 red bell pepper, seeded and sliced
◆ 1 yellow bell pepper, seeded and sliced
◆ 6 tbsp dry white wine

◆ 6 scallions, trimmed and diagonally sliced
◆ 4oz Parma ham, thinly sliced and cut into strips
◆ salt and ground black pepper
◆ 2 tbsp soured cream
◆ 2 tbsp chopped fresh basil

To serve

◆ 1lb fresh wholewheat spaghettini

Peel the ripe avocado, discard the seed, then blend in a food processor with the lemon juice. Scrape into a small bowl and cover with plastic wrap. Peel, discard the seed from the other avocado, and chop. Cover with plastic wrap and reserve both avocados.

Heat the oil in a pan and sauté the sliced tomatoes and peppers for 5 minutes, stirring frequently. Add the white wine and simmer gently for 3 minutes.

Add the scallions, the Parma ham, seasoning to taste, and sliced avocado to the pan. Blend the puréed avocado with the sour cream and stir into the pan. Heat through for 2-3 minutes, then stir in the basil. Cover with a lid, remove the pan from the heat, and keep warm while cooking the pasta.

Cook the spaghettini in plenty of salted boiling water for 1-2 minutes or until "al dente." Drain and return to the pan. Add the sauce to the pasta and toss lightly. Serve immediately.

Wholewheat Spaghettini with Avocado

SAFFRON FUSILLI WITH PEAS AND CHÈVRE

There are many different chèvres. Some are very salty and sharp while others are much milder and less salty. If you have not eaten chèvre before, choose one that is mild before you sample the sharper varieties.

NUTRITION FACTS

Serving size 1 (272g)

Calories 659	Calories from fat 297
	% daily value *
Total fat 33g	51%
Saturated fat 12g	58%
Monounsaturated fat 16.55g	0%
Polyunsaturated fat 2.54g	0%
Cholesterol 172mg	57%
Sodium 535mg	22%
Total carbohydrate 64g	21%
Dietary fiber 4g	15%
Sugars 3g	0%
Protein 25g	0%

* Percent daily values are based on a 2,000-calorie diet

For the sauce
- 4 tbsp olive oil
- 3-4 garlic cloves, peeled and sliced
- 1 large onion, peeled and sliced
- ½ cup dry white wine
- 2 cups snow peas, trimmed and halved

Heat the oil in a pan and sauté the garlic and onion for 5 minutes. Add the white wine, bring to a boil, and simmer for 3 minutes.

Blanch the snow peas in a pan of boiling water for 1 minute. Drain and refresh in cold water. Add to the pan with the diced herb-crushed chèvre. Heat through very gently for 3 minutes, stirring occasionally.

- 8oz herb-crushed chèvre, diced

To serve
- 1lb fresh saffron fusilli
- fresh flat leaf parsley sprigs

Meanwhile, cook the saffron fusilli in plenty of salted boiling water for 1-2 minutes or until "al dente." Drain and return to the pan. Add the snow peas and chèvre mixture. Toss lightly, garnish with the parsley, and then serve.

MUSHROOM TAGLIATELLE WITH SAUSAGE AND TOMATO

This recipe is based on the traditional English breakfast which is rapidly disappearing due to changing lifestyles and eating habits. This recipe is however, far healthier and, in my opinion, tastier.

NUTRITION FACTS

Serving size 1 (338g)

Calories 750	Calories from fat 360
	% daily value *
Total fat 40g	61%
Saturated fat 11g	56%
Monounsaturated fat 20.6g	0%
Polyunsaturated fat 4.59g	0%
Cholesterol 293mg	98%
Sodium 1193mg	50%
Total carbohydrate 68g	23%
Dietary fiber 4g	17%
Sugars 6g	0%
Protein 30g	0%

* Percent daily values are based on a 2,000-calorie diet

For the sauce
- 3 tbsp olive oil
- 1 onion, peeled and chopped
- 8oz pork sausage links, sliced
- 4 firm tomatoes, peeled, seeded, and chopped
- 2 tbsp chopped fresh flat leaf parsley

Heat the oil in a skillet and sauté the onion for 5 minutes or until softened. Add the sliced sausages and sauté for 2 more minutes. Stir in the tomatoes, cover with a lid, and remove from the heat. Reserve.

Meanwhile cook the mushroom tagliatelle in plenty of salted boiling water for 1-2 minutes or until "al dente." Drain and return to the pan.

- salt and ground black pepper
- 2 medium eggs

To serve
- 1lb fresh mushroom tagliatelle
- freshly shaved Romano cheese

Add the sausage mixture, parsley, and seasoning to taste, and stir lightly. Heat through for 1 minute then remove from the heat. Beat the eggs and stir into the pasta, letting the heat of the pasta cook the eggs. Once the eggs have cooked, serve topped with fresh shavings of cheese.

Saffron Fusilli with Peas and Chèvre

Black Spaghettini with Sautéed Shrimp

BLACK SPAGHETTINI WITH SAUTÉED SHRIMP

*The colors of this dish are simply stunning and, for even greater effect, choose carefully
the color of the plate you serve it on.*

For the sauce
- 3 tbsp olive oil
- 4 shallots, peeled and sliced into thin wedges
- 2-3 serrano or cayenne chiles, seeded and chopped
- 2-3 garlic cloves, peeled and thinly sliced
- 10oz large shrimp, shelled but tails left intact
- 1 cup snow peas, trimmed and cut in three

- 4 tbsp dry white wine
- grated rind of 1 lime
- 1 tbsp balsamic vinegar

To serve
- 1lb fresh black spaghettini
- lime rind and lime slices to garnish

Heat the oil in a pan and sauté the shallots, chiles, and garlic for 3 minutes. Add the shrimp and continue to sauté for 5 minutes or until the shrimp have just begun to turn pink.

Add the snow peas and wine and simmer for 2 minutes. Stir in the lime rind and balsamic vinegar. Cover with a lid, remove from the heat, and keep warm while cooking the pasta.

Cook the black spaghettini pasta in plenty of salted boiling water for 1 minute or until "al dente." Drain and return to the pan. Add the cooked shrimp and sauce, toss lightly, garnish and serve immediately.

NUTRITION FACTS

Serving size 1 (291g)
Calories 527   Calories from fat 162

	% daily value *
Total fat 18g	27%
Saturated fat 3g	15%
Monounsaturated fat 11.4g	0%
Polyunsaturated fat 1.9g	0%
Cholesterol 146mg	49%
Sodium 657mg	27%
Total carbohydrate 66g	22%
Dietary fiber 3g	13%
Sugars 4g	0%
Protein 23g	0%

* Percent daily values are based on a 2,000-calorie diet

TOMATO PAPPARDALLE WITH THREE CHEESES

*Here I have combined three of Italy's great cheeses to provide a quick and creamy sauce
with a subtle hint of lemon and parsley.*

For the sauce
- 4oz Gorgonzola cheese
- ¾ cup heavy whipping cream
- ½ cup freshly grated Parmesan cheese
- 4oz fontina cheese
- grated rind of 1 large lemon
- 2 tbsp chopped fresh flat leaf parsley
- ½ cup roughly chopped walnuts

To serve
- 1lb fresh tomato pappardalle
- sprigs of flat leaf parsley and zested lemon rind to garnish

Cut the Gorgonzola into small cubes and place in a saucepan with the heavy cream, Parmesan, and fontina cheese. Heat gently, stirring until completely melted.

Stir in the lemon rind with the chopped parsley and walnuts. Cover with a lid, remove from the heat, and keep warm.

Meanwhile, cook the tomato pappardalle in plenty of salted boiling water for 1-2 minutes or until "al dente." Drain and return to the pan. Add the cheese sauce, toss lightly, garnish, and serve immediately.

NUTRITION FACTS

Serving size 1 (263g)
Calories 804   Calories from fat 432

	% daily value *
Total fat 48g	74%
Saturated fat 24g	122%
Monounsaturated fat 13.7g	0%
Polyunsaturated fat 6.08g	0%
Cholesterol 277mg	92%
Sodium 922mg	38%
Total carbohydrate 63g	21%
Dietary fiber 2g	10%
Sugars 3g	0%
Protein 31g	0%

* Percent daily values are based on a 2,000-calorie diet

PASTA ROSSA WITH ASPARAGUS AND SMOKED HAM

Asparagus is delicious when lightly sautéed in a good oil and served "al dente."
Here the addition of the smoked ham gives this dish a slightly earthy flavor, which
combines well with the flavored pasta.

NUTRITION FACTS

Serving size 1 (324g)
Calories 687   Calories from fat 306

	% daily value *
Total fat 34g	52%
Saturated fat 10g	52%
Monounsaturated fat 17.7g	0%
Polyunsaturated fat 2.9g	0%
Cholesterol 200mg	67%
Sodium 1015mg	42%
Total carbohydrate 64g	21%
Dietary fiber 3g	12%
Sugars 4g	0%
Protein 27g	0%

* Percent daily values are based on a 2,000-calorie diet

For the sauce
- 4 tbsp olive oil
- 6 shallots, peeled and sliced
- 2 garlic cloves, peeled and minced
- 2 celery stems, trimmed and chopped
- small bunch baby asparagus, trimmed and cut in half
- ½ cup dry white wine

6oz smoked ham, cut into strips
- 4 tbsp mascarpone
- salt and ground black pepper
- 2 tbsp chopped flat leaf parsley

To serve
- 1lb fresh beet spaghetti
- sprigs of flat leaf parsley to garnish

Heat the oil in a pan and sauté the shallots, garlic, and celery for 5 minutes or until softened. Add the asparagus and sauté for 1 more minute.

Add the wine, bring to a boil, and simmer for 5 minutes or until the wine has been reduced by about half. Add the ham, cover with a lid, and remove from the heat.

Meanwhile, cook the beet spaghetti in plenty of boiling salted water for 1-2 minutes or until "al dente." Drain and return to the pan. Add the asparagus mixture to the beet spaghetti pasta with the mascarpone, seasoning, and parsley. Toss lightly until coated, garnish, and serve immediately.

MIXED HERB SPAGHETTI WITH MASCARPONE AND SPINACH

This creamy sauce is simple to make, delicious to eat, and is an ideal meal to serve
when you wish to impress but time is short.

NUTRITION FACTS

Serving size 1 (299g)
Calories 595   Calories from fat 234

	% daily value *
Total fat 26g	40%
Saturated fat 13g	66%
Monounsaturated fat 8.75g	0%
Polyunsaturated fat 1.84g	0%
Cholesterol 201mg	67%
Sodium 578mg	24%
Total carbohydrate 64g	21%
Dietary fiber 5g	21%
Sugars 3g	0%
Protein 27g	0%

* Percent daily values are based on a 2,000-calorie diet

For the sauce
- 2 tbsp butter
- 1 onion, peeled and chopped
- 2-3 smoked or regular garlic cloves, peeled and thinly sliced
- 1 red bell pepper, seeded and chopped
- 2 tbsp roughly chopped fresh thyme

8 cups fresh spinach, cleaned and shredded
- ¾ cup mascarpone cheese
- salt and ground black pepper
- ½-1 tsp grated nutmeg

To serve
- 1lb fresh mixed herb spaghetti

Melt the butter in a pan and sauté the onion and garlic for 5 minutes. Add the pepper and continue to sauté for 3 minutes. Stir in the thyme and spinach, and heat through for 5 minutes. Stir in the mascarpone cheese, seasoning to taste, and the nutmeg. Continue to

heat through gently for a further 3-5 minutes, until hot, stirring occasionally.

Meanwhile, cook the mixed herb spaghetti in plenty of salted boiling water for 1-2 minutes or until "al dente." Drain and return to the pan. Add the sauce, toss lightly, and serve.

CHAPTER EIGHT

SALADS

Here is a great selection of pasta salads to serve as snacks, lunches, even main meals. Different types of pasta are used and are combined with an exciting variety of ingredients and flavorful dressings. It is important to balance the shape and color of the pasta with the other ingredients to make the salad as attractive as possible.

PASTA AND WALDORF SALAD

This recipe is based on the famous Waldorf salad, of which every serious cook has their own interpretation. I would recommend that you try this salad as it gives an exciting new look to the original recipe.

NUTRITION FACTS

Serving size 1 (355g)
Calories 434   Calories from fat 162

	% daily value *
Total fat 18g	28%
Saturated fat 3g	16%
Monounsaturated fat 8.87g	0%
Polyunsaturated fat 4.35g	0%
Cholesterol 85mg	28%
Sodium 289mg	12%
Total carbohydrate 60g	20%
Dietary fiber 8g	30%
Sugars 20g	0%
Protein 12g	0%

* Percent daily values are based on a 2,000-calorie diet

For the salad
- 2 red apples, rinsed, cored and thinly sliced
- 2 ripe pears, rinsed, cored and sliced
- juice of 1 lemon
- 4 celery stems, trimmed and sliced
- ½ cup pecan halves
- 8oz fresh pasta, such as tricolored brandelle

Place the apples and pears in a bowl, pour over the lemon juice, and toss lightly. Add the sliced celery and pecan halves, and mix lightly.

Cook the pasta in plenty of salted boiling water for 1-2 minutes or until "al dente." Drain and add to the celery.

- 1 small head romaine lettuce
- freshly shaved Romano cheese

For the dressing
- 3 tbsp reduced calorie mayonnaise
- 2 tbsp thick, unflavored yogurt
- 1-2 tsp medium hot curry powder

Blend together the mayonnaise, yogurt, and curry powder to taste, reserve. Rinse the lettuce and use to line a salad bowl. Pile the prepared salad into the center and drizzle over the dressing. Sprinkle with the freshly shaved Romano cheese.

RAVIOLI SALAD

For this dish you do need good quality fresh flat leaf parsley, as the sprigs of parsley are encased in the pasta then cooked and tossed in a herb vinaigrette.

NUTRITION FACTS

Serving size 1 (127g)
Calories 414   Calories from fat 243

	% daily value *
Total fat 27g	42%
Saturated fat 5g	23%
Monounsaturated fat 18.1g	0%
Polyunsaturated fat 2.78g	0%
Cholesterol 189mg	63%
Sodium 750mg	31%
Total carbohydrate 30g	10%
Dietary fiber 1g	5%
Sugars 2g	0%
Protein 11g	0%

* Percent daily values are based on a 2,000-calorie diet

For the salad
- ½ batch basic pasta dough (see page 20)
- small bunch flat leaf parsley, rinsed
- 2oz can anchovy fillets, drained (and soaked, optional)
- 2 tbsp capers (soaked if preferred)
- 4 hard cooked eggs, shelled and sliced

Using your pasta machine, roll out the pasta dough to form strips about 5 inches wide. Place sprigs of the flat leaf parsley on half the dough, dampen edges, and fold over the other half of the pasta.

Using a fluted cutter, cut out squares ensuring that each square contains a sprig of parsley. Sprinkle with a little flour and let dry for about 1 hour.

For the dressing
- 6 tbsp extra virgin olive oil
- 2 garlic cloves, peeled and minced
- 2 shallots, peeled and finely chopped
- 1 tbsp chopped fresh flat leaf parsley
- 1 tbsp chopped fresh basil
- salt and ground black pepper
- 1 tbsp balsamic vinegar

For the salad dressing, heat the oil in a pan, and gently fry the garlic and shallots for 5 minutes or until softened. Remove the pan from the heat and stir in the herbs, seasoning, and vinegar. Cover and reserve.

Cook the ravioli squares in plenty of salted boiling water until "al dente." Drain and return to the pan. Pour over the prepared dressing and toss lightly. Arrange the ravioli in a warmed serving bowl. Top with the anchovy fillets, capers, and sliced hard cooked eggs, then serve.

Pasta and Waldorf Salad

FARFALLE WITH MARINATED BELL PEPPERS

Skinning the peppers before marinating ensures that the peppers absorb the marinade flavor quicker. The peppers are far easier to digest once skinned and the flesh is sweeter too.

For the salad
- 2 red bell peppers, seeded
- 2 yellow bell peppers, seeded
- 2 green bell peppers, seeded
- 6 tbsp olive oil
- 1-2 garlic cloves, peeled and minced
- 1 jalapeño chile, seeded and finely chopped
- 2 tbsp lemon juice
- grated rind of ½ lemon
- 1 tbsp chopped fresh basil
- 2 slices thick white bread

To serve
- salad greens
- 8oz fresh pasta, such as farfalle
- freshly shaved Parmesan cheese
- extra grated lemon rind

Preheat broiler to high and line the broiler rack with foil, or use a barbecue. Cut the peppers into quarters and place skin side up on the broiler rack. Broil for 10 minutes or until skins have blistered and blackened. Remove from the heat and place in a plastic bag and leave until cool.

Once cool, skin the peppers and slice thinly. Place the peppers in a shallow dish and pour over the oil. Sprinkle with the minced garlic, chile, lemon juice and rind, and basil. Cover and leave in the refrigerator for at least 2 hours, turning occasionally.

Cut the bread into cubes. Drain the peppers and reserve both peppers and marinade. Heat 3 tablespoons of the marinade in a skillet and fry the bread cubes until golden, stirring frequently. Drain on paper towels; reserve.

Cook the pasta in plenty of salted boiling water for 1-2 minutes or until "al dente." Drain and return to the pan. Mix the marinated peppers with the cooked pasta.

Arrange the salad greens in a serving bowl. Pile the pepper and pasta mix on top of the salad greens. Pour over the marinade and scatter over the croûtons. Serve with freshly shaved Parmesan cheese and grated lemon rind.

Farfalle with Marinated Peppers

Minty Crab, Pear and Pasta Salad

MINTY CRAB, PEAR, AND PASTA SALAD

I found the dressing used in this recipe while looking through an old cookbook. I have updated it by using a flavored vinegar and oil, and I am sure that once you have tried this recipe it will quickly become a firm favorite.

For the salad
- 8oz cooked fresh pasta, such as tricolored spaghetti
- 7oz white crab meat, flaked
- 2 oranges, peeled and cut into sections
- 2 pink grapefruit, peeled and cut into sections
- 2 tbsp chopped fresh mint
- ½ cup pecan halves

Place the cooked pasta in a bowl and add the flaked crab meat, orange and grapefruit sections, chopped mint, and pecan halves. Toss lightly and spoon into a serving bowl.

For the dressing
- 2 ripe pears
- ½ cup walnut oil
- 4 tbsp extra virgin olive oil
- 1 tbsp orange or raspberry vinegar
- salt and ground black pepper

For the dressing, peel and core the pears, then place in a food processor. Gradually blend the pears with the walnut oil and then the olive oil. Add the vinegar with seasoning and blend for 30 seconds or until smooth. Pour over the salad, toss lightly, and serve.

NUTRITION FACTS

Serving size 1 (440g)
Calories 693   Calories from fat 468

	% daily value *
Total fat 52g	80%
Saturated fat 5g	27%
Monounsaturated fat 22.2g	0%
Polyunsaturated fat 21.7g	0%
Cholesterol 68mg	23%
Sodium 398mg	17%
Total carbohydrate 47g	16%
Dietary fiber 6g	24%
Sugars 24g	0%
Protein 14g	0%

* Percent daily values are based on a 2,000-calorie diet

PASTA AND YOGURT SALAD

There are many different ingredients that can be used as salad dressings. Yogurt makes an ideal base for a salad dressing, and with more people watching their intake of fat, yogurt is an obvious choice.

For the salad
- 2 oranges
- 1 tbsp olive oil
- 2 cups sliced leeks
- ¼ cup pine nuts
- 2 tbsp roughly chopped fresh flat leaf parsley
- 1 cup broccoli flowerets
- 1 cup chopped young carrots
- 4oz mortadella, sliced into strips
- ⅔ cup low-fat plain yogurt
- salt and ground black pepper
- radicchio leaves

To serve
- 8oz fresh pasta, such as tricolored farfalle

Remove the rind from one of the oranges, then peel and divide both oranges into sections. Reserve rind and orange sections.

Heat the oil in a skillet and sauté the leeks for 5 minutes or until just softened. Add the orange rind and pine nuts, and continue to sauté for 2 minutes. Remove from the heat, stir in the parsley, and place in a bowl.

Divide the broccoli into smaller flowerets and blanch in lightly salted boiling water for 2 minutes. Drain and plunge into cold water. Drain again, and add to the leeks.

Cook the carrots in lightly salted boiling water for 5 minutes or until just cooked. Drain and add to the vegetables.

Cook the pasta in plenty of salted boiling water for 1-2 minutes or until "al dente." Drain and return to the pan.

Add the mortadella to the pasta with the vegetables and orange sections. Stir in the yogurt with seasoning to taste. Mix lightly together. Line a serving bowl with the radicchio leaves. Spoon the salad into the bowl and serve.

NUTRITION FACTS

Serving size 1 (312g)
Calories 430   Calories from fat 162

	% daily value *
Total fat 18g	28%
Saturated fat 5g	24%
Monounsaturated fat 8.87g	0%
Polyunsaturated fat 2.97g	0%
Cholesterol 93mg	31%
Sodium 653mg	27%
Total carbohydrate 53g	18%
Dietary fiber 5g	22%
Sugars 13g	0%
Protein 16g	0%

* Percent daily values are based on a 2,000-calorie diet

FARFALLE AND MIXED VEGETABLE MEDLEY

*When cooking pasta, you may find that sometimes you have leftover pasta.
This is ideal to use as the basis of a delicious salad. The short pastas and shapes
are better suited.*

NUTRITION FACTS

Serving size 1 (238g)

Calories 201	Calories from fat 45

	% daily value *
Total fat 5g	8%
Saturated fat 1g	4%
Monounsaturated fat 1.1g	0%
Polyunsaturated fat 2.66g	0%
Cholesterol 28mg	9%
Sodium 307mg	13%
Total carbohydrate 34g	11%
Dietary fiber 2g	9%
Sugars 3g	0%
Protein 7g	0%

** Percent daily values are based on a
2,000-calorie diet*

For the salad
- 1 cup snow peas
- 6 scallions, trimmed
- 1 small bunch radishes, trimmed
- ¾ cup canned baby corn
- 1 cup cherry tomatoes
- 2oz arugula, rinsed
- 10oz cooked fresh farfalle

For the dressing
- 5 tbsp reduced calorie mayonnaise
- 3 tbsp lemon juice
- 2 tbsp chopped fresh basil

Cut the snow peas in half, then blanch in lightly salted boiling water for 1 minute. Drain and plunge into cold water, drain again, and place in a serving bowl.

Slice the scallions diagonally and add to the peas. Cut about 4-5 radishes into roses if liked and leave in cold water to open. Slice the remaining radishes and add to the bowl. Cut the baby corn and tomatoes in half; add to the bowl with the arugula and cooked farfalle. Toss ingredients lightly together.

Place the dressing ingredients in a screw top jar and shake vigorously. Pour over the salad, toss lightly, and serve garnished with the radish roses.

CORONATION TURKEY PASTA

This makes a delicious, filling salad. Ideal for entertaining or for when a more substantial meal is required.

For the dressing
- 2 tbsp olive oil
- 1 small onion
- 1 tbsp medium hot curry powder
- ⅔ cup dry white wine
- ½ cup ready-to-eat dried apricots, chopped
- 4 tbsp reduced-calorie mayonnaise
- 2 tbsp sour cream

For the salad
- 8oz diced cooked turkey meat
- 10oz cooked fresh pasta, such as brandelle
- ¼ cup sliced toasted almonds
- salad greens
- fresh apricot slices

For the salad dressing, heat the olive oil in a pan and gently sauté the onion for 5 minutes or until softened. Add the medium hot curry powder and sauté for 2 minutes, stirring frequently. Pour in the dry white wine with 3 tablespoons of water, add the chopped apricots, and simmer gently for 10 minutes or until the apricots are soft and pulpy.

Remove from the heat and blend in a food processor to form a smooth purée. Mix the mayonnaise, sour cream, and apricot purée together. Stir the diced turkey meat, cooked pasta, and almonds into the dressing.

Arrange the salad greens in the base of a serving platter, then pile the pasta mixture on top. Garnish with the apricot slices and serve.

NUTRITION FACTS

Serving size 1 (245g)
Calories 349   Calories from fat 153

	% daily value *
Total fat 17g	26%
Saturated fat 3g	16%
Monounsaturated fat 8.69g	0%
Polyunsaturated fat 3.71g	0%
Cholesterol 55mg	18%
Sodium 217mg	9%
Total carbohydrate 33g	11%
Dietary fiber 3g	12%
Sugars 9g	0%
Protein 17g	0%

* Percent daily values are based on a 2,000-calorie diet

PASTA NIÇOISE WITH BALSAMIC DRESSING

Since discovering balsamic vinegar, my salads have reached new heights in gastronomic experience. I would urge anyone who has not tried this vinegar to do so immediately.

For the salad
- 6oz French green beans, trimmed
- 7oz can tuna, drained
- 10oz cooked fresh pasta, such as fusilli
- 2 tbsp chopped fresh flat leaf parsley
- 2 large tomatoes, sliced
- 2 medium hard cooked eggs, shelled and sliced
- 2oz can anchovy fillets, drained (soaked if preferred)
- ⅓ cup pitted black olives

For the dressing
- 5 tbsp extra virgin olive oil
- 1 tsp liquid honey
- 1 tsp wholegrain mustard
- salt and ground black pepper
- 2 tbsp balsamic vinegar

Cook the French green beans in a pan of lightly salted boiling water for 4-5 minutes or until just cooked. Drain and plunge into cold water. Drain again and reserve. Divide the drained tuna into small chunks.

Mix the pasta and chopped parsley together and place in the base of a shallow serving platter

or dish. Arrange the cooked beans, sliced tomatoes, tuna, eggs, drained anchovies, and olives attractively on top of the pasta.

Place the dressing ingredients in a screw top jar and shake vigorously. Pour over the salad just before serving.

NUTRITION FACTS

Serving size 1 (293g)
Calories 510   Calories from fat 243

	% daily value *
Total fat 27g	41%
Saturated fat 4g	21%
Monounsaturated fat 16.0g	0%
Polyunsaturated fat 2.74g	0%
Cholesterol 224mg	75%
Sodium 1363mg	57%
Total carbohydrate 38g	13%
Dietary fiber 2g	10%
Sugars 6g	0%
Protein 28g	0%

* Percent daily values are based on a 2,000-calorie diet

MELON, SMOKED CHICKEN, AND PASTA SALAD

Use a selection of melons in this refreshing salad. The different colors of the melons make this an attractive dish.

NUTRITION FACTS

Serving size 1 (294g)
Calories 285   Calories from fat 153

	% daily value *
Total fat 17g	26%
Saturated fat 4g	22%
Monounsaturated fat 9.5g	0%
Polyunsaturated fat 1.6g	0%
Cholesterol 46mg	15%
Sodium 96mg	4%
Total carbohydrate 16g	5%
Dietary fiber 2g	10%
Sugars 12g	0%
Protein 17g	0%

* Percent daily values are based on a 2,000-calorie diet

For the salad
- 12oz assorted melon slices
- 6oz smoked chicken meat
- 8oz cooked fresh mushroom pasta
- 1 large orange, peeled and segmented
- fresh spinach leaves
- 2 tbsp grated Gruyère cheese
- orange rind to garnish

Discard the seeds and skin from the melons and cut into small dice. Place in a bowl.

Cut the smoked chicken into strips and add to the melon with the pasta and orange segments; mix lightly. Arrange the fresh spinach leaves on a serving platter.

For the dressing
- 4 tbsp sour cream
- 1 tsp wholegrain mustard
- 3 tbsp extra virgin olive oil
- 2 tbsp champagne or white wine vinegar

For the dressing, place the sour cream in a bowl and beat in the mustard. Gradually beat in the olive oil, then the vinegar. Spoon the pasta onto the spinach lined platter, sprinkle with the grated cheese, garnish, and serve. Hand the dressing separately.

SMOKED SALMON, PASTA, AND RASPBERRY SALAD

I personally love the combination of sweet and savory, especially if the sweet food is fruit. Here, sweet ripe raspberries are used with smoked salmon to give an interesting and stunning taste sensation.

NUTRITION FACTS

Serving size 1 (182g)
Calories 412   Calories from fat 216

	% daily value *
Total fat 24g	37%
Saturated fat 6g	29%
Monounsaturated fat 12.2g	0%
Polyunsaturated fat 4.09g	0%
Cholesterol 95mg	32%
Sodium 418mg	17%
Total carbohydrate 34g	12%
Dietary fiber 3g	13%
Sugars 4g	0%
Protein 15g	0%

* Percent daily values are based on a 2,000-calorie diet

For the dressing
- 4 tbsp raspberry vinegar
- 3 tbsp extra virgin olive oil
- 1 tbsp walnut oil
- pinch of mustard powder
- 4 tbsp sour cream

For the dressing, blend the vinegar with the oils and mustard powder until thoroughly mixed, then stir in the sour cream. Cover and leave in the refrigerator for 30 minutes.

Cook the pasta in plenty of salted boiling water for 1-2 minutes or until "al dente." Drain and return to the pan.

For the salad
- 8oz fresh pasta, such as mixed herb fusilli
- 6 scallions, trimmed
- 4oz smoked salmon
- 1 cup fresh raspberries
- 1 cup watercress sprigs, rinsed
- freshly shaved Romano cheese

Meanwhile, diagonally slice the scallions, cut the smoked salmon into strips, and pick over the fresh raspberries. Add the scallions, smoked salmon, raspberries, and watercress sprigs to the cooked pasta. Add the salad dressing and toss lightly. Serve, sprinkled with the freshly shaved cheese.

Melon, Smoked Chicken, and Pasta Salad

FIG, PASTA, AND PROSCIUTTO SALAD

Make the most of fresh figs when they are available. Whether it is the green or purple variety, their soft flesh, delicate flavor, and attractive appearance make them an ideal salad ingredient.

For the salad
- 3-inch piece cucumber
- salt
- 4oz prosciutto, sliced
- 2 ripe pears
- 1 tbsp orange juice
- small bunch arugula
- 8oz cooked fresh pasta, such as fusilli
- 4 fresh ripe figs

- edible flowers such as pansies, nasturtians, and primroses (optional)

For the dressing
- 3 tbsp orange juice
- 4 tbsp extra virgin olive oil
- 1 tsp liquid honey
- 1-2 tsp Dijon-style mustard
- ground black pepper

Peel the cucumber and slice thinly. Sprinkle with salt and leave for 30 minutes. Rinse well in cold water and pat dry with paper towels. Place in a bowl with the prosciutto.

Rinse the ripe pears and peel if preferred. Core and slice thinly. Sprinkle with the fresh orange juice and add to the bowl. Tear the arugula into small pieces if large leaves and add

to the bowl with the cooked pasta. Toss lightly together until mixed.

Slice the figs and add to the bowl. Spoon onto a serving platter.

Place the dressing ingredients into a screw top jar and shake vigorously until well blended. Pour over the pasta. Garnish the salad with the edible flowers and serve.

PASTA WITH TOMATO TAPENADE

Tapenade can be found throughout the Mediterranean and is delicious spread on toast as a tasty snack. It also can form the basis of an interesting salad, as this recipe illustrates.

For the tapenade
- 1⅓ cups black olives, pitted
- 6 sun-dried tomatoes
- 1½oz capers (soaked if preferred)
- 1 tbsp chopped fresh parsley
- 2 garlic cloves, peeled and minced
- 1 tsp wholegrain mustard
- 2oz can anchovy fillets (soaked if preferred)
- ⅔ cup extra virgin olive oil
- ground black pepper

To serve
- 8oz fresh pasta, such as mixed herb farfalle
- romaine lettuce
- sprigs of watercress
- 2 tbsp freshly made croûtons
- ½ cup halved cherry tomatoes

For the tomato tapenade, blend the black olives, sun-dried tomatoes, capers, chopped fresh parsley, garlic, wholegrain mustard, and anchovies with their oil to a thick paste in a food processor. With the motor still running, gradually pour in the olive oil in a thin steady stream to form a thick purée. Add black pepper to taste and reserve.

Cook the pasta in plenty of salted boiling water for 1-2 minutes or until "al dente." Drain and return to the pan.

Meanwhile, rinse the lettuce and watercress leaves and use to line a salad bowl. Add the tapenade to the pasta and toss lightly. Serve in the lettuce-lined bowl, sprinkled with the croûtons. Garnish with the cherry tomatoes.

Fig, Pasta, and Prosciutto Salad

Wild Mushroom and Pasta Salad

WILD MUSHROOM AND PASTA SALAD

For a more substantial salad, add some shelled shrimp or a mixture of seafood.

For the salad
- ½ cup virgin olive oil
- 4 shallots, peeled and sliced
- 2-3 garlic cloves, peeled and sliced
- 1-2 serrano chiles, seeded and sliced
- 4 sun-dried tomatoes, chopped
- 2½ cups assorted wild mushrooms, such as oyster or chanterelle, wiped and sliced
- 4 tbsp dry white wine
- salt and ground black pepper
- 1-2 tsp truffle oil
- assorted bitter salad greens, such as arugula, spinach, watercress, or sorrel

To serve
- 8oz fresh rigatoni
- few shavings black truffle (optional)
- sprigs flat leaf parsley to garnish

Heat the oil in a skillet and sauté the shallots, garlic, and chiles for 2 minutes. Add the sun-dried tomatoes and mushrooms; continue to sauté for 3 more minutes. Add the white wine and seasoning; simmer for 3-4 minutes or until the mushrooms are just tender.

Cook the pasta in plenty of salted boiling water for 1-2 minutes or until "al dente." Drain and return to the pan. Add the truffle oil to the pasta and heat through for 1 minute, stirring lightly. Stir in the sautéed mushroom mixture.

Line a salad bowl with the salad greens and spoon the pasta salad on top. Sprinkle with the freshly shaved truffle, if used, garnish, and serve.

NUTRITION FACTS

Serving size 1 (171g)	
Calories 464	Calories from fat 288

	% daily value *
Total fat 32g	50%
Saturated fat 5g	23%
Monounsaturated fat 22.7g	0%
Polyunsaturated fat 3g	0%
Cholesterol 75mg	25%
Sodium 260mg	11%
Total carbohydrate 35g	12%
Dietary fiber 2g	9%
Sugars 2g	0%
Protein 8g	0%

* Percent daily values are based on a 2,000-calorie diet

PASTA AND DUCK SALAD

This flavorful salad is ideal for using up leftover roast duck. If you prefer, you can pan-fry duck breasts, drain thoroughly, then slice.

- 8oz fresh farfalle
- 4 tbsp virgin olive oil
- 4oz pancetta or smoked bacon, rinded and cut into strips
- 3 tbsp dry white wine
- 1 tbsp white wine vinegar
- salt and ground black pepper
- 8oz roast duck, cut into strips
- 1 cup diced Gruyère cheese
- 1 large orange, peeled and cut into sections
- roughly chopped fresh flat leaf parsley
- salad greens
- halved kumquats (optional) to garnish

Cook the farfalle in salted boiling water for 1-2 minutes or until "al dente." Drain and place in a bowl. Pour over the olive oil and toss lightly.

Meanwhile, place the pancetta or bacon in a non-stick skillet and cook gently until crisp. Add the white wine and vinegar and simmer for 2 minutes, stirring occasionally.

Add the pancetta and liquid to the pasta with seasoning to taste, the duck strips, Gruyère cheese, orange sections, and chopped parsley. Toss lightly.

Arrange the salad greens on a platter and spoon on the pasta mixture. Garnish with the kumquat halves and serve.

NUTRITION FACTS

Serving size 1 (273g)	
Calories 691	Calories from fat 405

	% daily value *
Total fat 45g	69%
Saturated fat 14g	70%
Monounsaturated fat 23g	0%
Polyunsaturated fat 4.5g	0%
Cholesterol 173mg	58%
Sodium 820mg	34%
Total carbohydrate 34g	12%
Dietary fiber 2g	7%
Sugars 4g	0%
Protein 35g	0%

* Percent daily values are based on a 2,000-calorie diet

WARM AVOCADO, PARMA HAM, AND PASTA SALAD

One of the joys of eating is the wide range of ingredients from all over the world which are so readily available to so many of us. This recipe includes ingredients that have been produced continents apart and yet the flavors balance harmoniously.

NUTRITION FACTS

Serving size 1 (332g)
Calories 675   Calories from fat 414

	% daily value *
Total fat 46g	71%
Saturated fat 7g	35%
Monounsaturated fat 28.6g	0%
Polyunsaturated fat 7.54g	0%
Cholesterol 91mg	30%
Sodium 632mg	26%
Total carbohydrate 53g	18%
Dietary fiber 12g	50%
Sugars 6g	0%
Protein 18g	0%

* Percent daily values are based on a 2,000-calorie diet

For the salad
- 2 ripe but firm avocados
- 3 tbsp lime juice
- 4 tbsp extra virgin olive oil
- 1 red onion, peeled and cut into thin wedges
- ¾ cup pecan halves
- 1 tbsp maple syrup

- 4oz Parma ham, snipped into strips
- salt and ground black pepper
- red and green endive leaves

To serve
- 8oz fresh pasta, such as brandelle
- sprigs of flat leaf parsley

Peel the avocados, discard the seeds, and dice the flesh. Place in a bowl and sprinkle with the lime juice, reserve.

Heat the oil in a skillet and sauté the onion briskly until the edges are slightly blackened. Reduce the heat, add the pecans, and sauté for 1 minute. Remove from the heat and add the avocado with the lime juice, maple syrup, and Parma ham, and heat through for 2 minutes.

Cook the pasta in plenty of salted boiling water for 1-2 minutes or until "al dente." Drain and return to the pan. Pour over the avocado and ham mixture; add seasoning to taste. Heat through for 2 minutes, stirring lightly.

Meanwhile, line a serving platter with the red and green endive leaves and pile the pasta mixture on top. Garnish with the parsley sprigs.

PARSLEY AND LEMON PASTA

This salad is quick, simple to prepare, and delicious to eat. It makes a refreshing change when you are searching for a new taste experience.

NUTRITION FACTS

Serving size 1 (138g)
Calories 349   Calories from fat 162

	% daily value *
Total fat 18g	28%
Saturated fat 3g	15%
Monounsaturated fat 11.1g	0%
Polyunsaturated fat 3.01g	0%
Cholesterol 83mg	28%
Sodium 947mg	39%
Total carbohydrate 34g	11%
Dietary fiber 2g	9%
Sugars 2g	0%
Protein 13g	0%

* Percent daily values are based on a 2,000-calorie diet

For the dressing
- 2 tbsp chopped fresh flat leaf parsley
- 1 tbsp chopped fresh mint
- grated rind of 1 lemon
- 2 garlic cloves, peeled and minced
- 3 tbsp extra virgin olive oil
- 6 tbsp thick, unflavored yogurt
- 2-3 tbsp toasted pine nuts
- salt and ground black pepper

For the salad
- 8oz fresh pasta, such as mushroom fusilli
- 1 cup baby spinach leaves, rinsed
- 2 tbsp capers (soaked if preferred)
- 2oz can anchovy fillets, drained (soaked if preferred)

Blend the parsley, mint, lemon rind, garlic, and oil together in a food processor to form a thick paste. With the motor still running, gradually blend in the yogurt to form a thick mayonnaise-style dressing. Scrape the yogurt mixture into a bowl and stir in the pine nuts with seasoning to taste. Reserve.

Meanwhile, cook the pasta in plenty of boiling salted water for 1-2 minutes or until "al dente." Drain and return to the pan. Add the dressing and stir until lightly coated.

Arrange the spinach leaves in a bowl and spoon the pasta on top. Sprinkle with the capers, arrange the anchovies on top, then serve.

CHAPTER NINE

DESSERTS

Although pasta is mainly a savory ingredient, it is often used in desserts. Here, I have combined the pasta with various ingredients to create some stunning and unusual sweet recipes; from Sweet Fettuccine with Maple Syrup to Oranges with Chocolate Ribbons. If you plan to indulge in a pasta dessert, you should serve a lighter main course.

ORANGES WITH CHOCOLATE RIBBONS

I have to admit to a passion for chocolate. Here I have combined it with oranges that have been marinated in brandy, providing a simple yet exotic dessert, suitable for any dinner party or special occasion.

- 4 large oranges
- ¼ cup sugar
- 2-3 tbsp brandy
- 2-3 whole cloves
- 8oz chocolate fettuccine
- 1 tbsp sliced toasted almonds
- 1 tbsp confectioners' sugar, sifted
- lightly whipped heavy cream or thick, unflavored yogurt

Peel the oranges, taking care to remove all the bitter white pith. Slice thinly and place in a glass mixing bowl.

Dissolve the sugar with ⅔ cup water in a heavy pan over moderate heat. Once dissolved, bring to a boil and boil for 5 minutes or until a light sugar syrup is formed.

Remove from the heat and stir in the brandy and cloves. Pour over the oranges. Leave for at least 2 hours, turning the oranges occasionally in the marinade.

Cook the chocolate fettuccine in plenty of boiling water for 1-2 minutes or until "al dente," then drain. Arrange on four individual serving plates. Spoon the oranges over the pasta and sprinkle with the sliced toasted almonds, toss lightly, and sprinkle with confectioners' sugar. Serve with the cream or yogurt.

CHOCOLATE SPIRALS WITH PISTACHIO AND ROSE CREAM

Stirred into freshly whipped cream, rose water gives a lightly perfumed and fragrant cream which combines well with the raspberries and chocolate in this recipe.

For the dessert
- ¼ cup unsalted shelled pistachio nuts
- ⅔ cup heavy whipping cream
- 1 tbsp rose water
- 2 cups fresh raspberries
- 8oz fresh chocolate tagliatelle

To decorate
- rose petals

Preheat the oven to 400°F and roast the pistachio nuts for 10 minutes. Remove from the oven, cool, and roughly chop.

Whip the cream lightly, stir in the rose water, and chill until required. Clean the raspberries, rinsing lightly, and dry on paper towels.

Cook the chocolate tagliatelle in plenty of boiling water for 1-2 minutes or until "al dente." Drain and stir in the cream. Arrange the pasta in small nests with the raspberries. Scatter with the chopped pistachios and decorate with rose petals. Serve immediately.

Oranges with Chocolate Ribbons

Sweet Fettuccine with Maple Syrup

SWEET FETTUCCINE WITH MAPLE SYRUP

When using pasta for desserts, cook the pasta in unsalted water, then toss the cooked pasta in melted butter. Here I have used some toasted nuts to serve with the pasta and poured over maple syrup—certainly not for serious weight watchers!

For the dessert
- 1 cup mixed shelled nuts, such as pecan halves, skinned hazelnuts, and blanched almonds
- 4 tbsp unsalted butter, melted
- 1 tsp ground cinnamon
- 4 tbsp maple syrup
- 8oz fresh fettuccine

To decorate
- fresh strawberries
- sprigs of mint

Preheat the oven to 400°F and roast the nuts for 10 minutes or until golden. Remove from the oven and cool.

Melt the unsalted butter in a pan and stir in the ground cinnamon, maple syrup, and roasted mixed nuts.

Meanwhile, cook the fettuccine in plenty of boiling water for 1-2 minutes or until "al dente." Drain and return to the pan. Pour over the maple syrup and nut sauce and toss lightly. Serve immediately decorated with the strawberries, cut into fans and mint sprigs.

NUTRITION FACTS

Serving size 1 (146g)
Calories 544   Calories from fat 306

	% daily value *
Total fat 34g	52%
Saturated fat 11g	54%
Monounsaturated fat 16.3g	0%
Polyunsaturated fat 4.74g	0%
Cholesterol 108mg	36%
Sodium 106mg	4%
Total carbohydrate 52g	17%
Dietary fiber 5g	19%
Sugars 15g	0%
Protein 12g	0%

* Percent daily values are based on a 2,000-calorie diet

FARFALLE WITH CARDAMOM

Vanilla flavored superfine sugar is easily prepared. Simply place 1-2 vanilla beans in a screw-top jar, fill with superfine sugar, and leave for 2 weeks. Keep topping up the sugar after use; then it can be used for months.

- 2½ cups skim milk
- 1 medium egg
- ¼ cup vanilla flavored superfine sugar

- 6 cardamom pods, split
- 8oz fresh farfalle, dried
- 2 tbsp butter

Preheat the oven to 325°F and lightly butter an ovenproof dish. Warm the skim milk. Beat the egg with the vanilla flavored superfine sugar, then gradually beat in the warmed milk. Add the cardamom pods.

Place the farfalle in the buttered ovenproof dish and pour over the milk mixture. Dot with small pieces of butter. Bake in the oven for about 45 minutes or until the pasta is cooked, stirring occasionally. Serve warm.

NUTRITION FACTS

Serving size 1 (244g)
Calories 356   Calories from fat 108

	% daily value *
Total fat 12g	18%
Saturated fat 5g	26%
Monounsaturated fat 4.32g	0%
Polyunsaturated fat 0.96g	0%
Cholesterol 147mg	49%
Sodium 255mg	11%
Total carbohydrate 50g	17%
Dietary fiber 1g	4%
Sugars 20g	0%
Protein 13g	0%

* Percent daily values are based on a 2,000-calorie diet

ORANGE ANGEL HAIR WITH FRUITS

If preferred you can use an unflavored pasta for this dish; alternatively, try using a chocolate pasta. When making flavored pastas, it is an excellent idea to make double the quantity and store half for later use.

NUTRITION FACTS

Serving size 1 (129g)
Calories 352   Calories from fat 108

	% daily value *
Total fat 12g	19%
Saturated fat 7g	33%
Monounsaturated fat 4.13g	0%
Polyunsaturated fat 0.83g	0%
Cholesterol 115mg	38%
Sodium 161mg	7%
Total carbohydrate 57g	19%
Dietary fiber 2g	8%
Sugars 17g	0%
Protein 5g	0%

* Percent daily values are based on a 2,000-calorie diet

- 4oz orange angel hair pasta
- 1 medium egg
- 2 tbsp liquid honey, or to taste
- ½ tsp ground cinnamon
- 3 tbsp butter, melted
- ⅓ cup raisins
- ½ cup chopped candied cherries
- ½ cup candied angelica or other candied fruits, chopped
- 1-2 tsp confectioners' sugar, sifted

Preheat the oven to 400°F and lightly butter an ovenproof dish. Cook the angel hair pasta in plenty of boiling water for 1 minute or until "al dente." Drain, rinse under hot water, and thoroughly drain.

Beat the egg with the honey and cinnamon. Stir in the drained pasta and melted butter. Mix the raisins, cherries, and angelica together.

Spoon half the pasta mixture into the base of the buttered dish and cover with the raisin mixture. Top with the remaining pasta mixture. Bake in the oven for 25 minutes. Serve warm sprinkled with confectioners' sugar.

COCONUT SPAGHETTINI

This recipe is based on a traditional Indian dessert, normally served at the end of the Ramadan fast. It is delicately flavored with rose water and cardamom.

NUTRITION FACTS

Serving size 1 (270g)
Calories 399   Calories from fat 162

	% daily value *
Total fat 18g	27%
Saturated fat 10g	51%
Monounsaturated fat 5.0g	0%
Polyunsaturated fat 1.4g	0%
Cholesterol 44mg	15%
Sodium 127mg	5%
Total carbohydrate 53g	18%
Dietary fiber 3g	13%
Sugars 38g	0%
Protein 11g	0%

* Percent daily values are based on a 2,000-calorie diet

- 2½ cups milk
- 2 green cardamom pods, split
- 1 tbsp rose water
- 3oz fresh spaghettini
- 4 tbsp liquid honey
- 1⅓ cups shredded coconut
- ¼ cup sliced almonds
- ⅓ cup ready-to-eat dried apricots, finely chopped
- 2-3 tbsp heavy whipping cream

Place the milk and cardamom pods in a pan and bring to a boil. Reduce the heat and simmer very gently for 10 minutes; stir occasionally. Take care that the mixture does not burn.

Add the rose water and spaghettini to the milk and stir for a few minutes. Simmer for about 8 minutes, then add the honey. Increase

Stir in the coconut, almonds, and apricots, and continue to simmer for 20 minutes, stirring occasionally until the mixture is thick and creamy. Discard the cardamom pods, stir in cream, heat for 1 minute and serve warm.

Orange Angel Hair with Fruits

APR 23 2002 DA
128

INDEX